RENATE BEIGEL has spent many years in the lighting industry and is well aware that eighty percent of all decisions about selecting the lighting for the family home are made by women. She has therefore ensured that Part 1 of this book is easily understood by house-wives and homemakers.

STANLEY LYONS, also with a long career in lighting, has written many books on the subject. His approach is to take the reader from first principles to a useful level of practical knowledge. While he advises where professional help with electrical installation work should be sought, he has ensured that the tasks described in Part 2 of this book are within the scope of the DIY handyman.

This book has been prepared in co-operation with
The Lighting Association Ltd.

LIGHTING YOUR HOME

Ideas for Homemakers plus DIY Guidance

RENATE BEIGEL AND STANLEY LYONS

Quiller Press

First published 1994 by Quiller Press Limited,
46 Lillie Road, London SW6 1TN

ISBN 1 870948 94 7

© Stanley Lyons 1994

Designed by Tim McPhee
Produced by Book Production Consultants Plc, Cambridge
Colour reproduction by Hilo Offset, Colchester, Essex
Printed by Toppan Printing Co Ltd, Singapore

Contents

Preface

This is a book for everyone who wants to know how to provide attractive, pleasant and economical lighting in their home.

Because it is written to suit the needs of a wide readership, this book contains rather more technical facts than are usually provided in books intended for the general public. But the non-technical domestic reader should not be frightened off, for most of these ideas are easier to understand than they may at first seem. Even if you do not read some of the more technical questions and answers, you will still learn the principles of how to achieve better lighting for your home with economy and safety.

To simplify the presentation of a lot of useful facts, it is written in two parts.

Part 1 (Chapters 1 to 8) is about choosing the sort of lighting you want, and will be easily understood by anyone who has no technical knowledge of lighting or electricity. It describes how to apply the principles of good lighting in your home, and indicates which kinds of lamps and lighting fittings are appropriate for each application.

Part 2 (Chapters 9 to 16) is intended for those who want to know 'why' as well as 'how'. It explains and expands many of the facts given in Part 1, and contains practical guidelines on installing lighting which will be helpful to those who want to improve their lighting by DIY.

PART 1

BASIC IDEAS ABOUT GOOD LIGHTING FOR EVERYONE

This part contains basic ideas for everyone about how to light your home well. You do not need to have any technical knowledge, nor be a DIY expert, in order to be able to understand it.

INTRODUCTION

Why is good lighting in the home important?

Of all the factors that combine to make one's home comfortable, welcoming and safe, lighting is the feature that can most readily and economically be adjusted to suit our tastes and needs. Sadly, many people neglect their lighting, giving it little thought beyond replacing failed bulbs. Yet, with a little imagination and quite moderate expenditure, they could have lighting that is kind to their eyes, which creates a good atmosphere by enhancing the decor and comfort of their surroundings, and which will be admired as evidence of the pride they take in their homes.

Most homemakers select their curtains, carpets and furnishings with care, and take pains to make their homes comfortable. Yet many neglect to provide the lighting that would literally show their homes and themselves in the best light. Good lighting can enhance the comfort and safety of our homes. It is possible to transform rooms by providing appropriate lighting, and at far less cost than might at first be thought. Indeed, by applying the ideas you will find in this book, you may make savings in the cost of lighting your home. Good lighting will produce the right visual conditions for activities such as children's homework, cooking, reading in bed, watching television, and for creating the appropriate atmosphere for social occasions.

What are the benefits of good lighting in the home?

- *Visual comfort.* Perhaps the most important benefit of having good lighting is visual comfort. This means that you will enjoy the pleasure of being in a tastefully well-lit environment, with the benefit of being able to see clearly when performing tasks such as cooking, reading or hobbies. Lighting can be arranged so as not to produce excessive glare, and with the minimum of annoying reflections – for example, from the screen of the television or your home computer.

LEFT: Recessed lighting is unobtrusive; the addition of strategically placed lights, such as table or floor standards (or even candles!) will highlight and sculpture the special features of the room.

- *Ease in doing difficult visual tasks.* Sufficient and suitable lighting enables things to be done without strain, and without one having to take up a tiring, uncomfortable posture in order to bring one's eyes nearer to the task. Hobbies, such as embroidery, quilting and stamp collecting, become much more enjoyable when one can see the details of the objects clearly. Older people, and persons with a visual handicap particularly, benefit from the provision of plenty of light on their tasks. Good lighting protects children's eyesight when doing homework and hobbies.

- *Safety.* Lighting makes an important contribution to safety, particularly in the kitchen and on the stairs, and possibly outdoors, too.

- *Style and good decor.* Choose your lighting fittings with care, and exercise good taste. Then you will create lighting that not only functions well but also looks good!

LEFT: Carefully planned lighting can create dramatic contrasts of mood, and impart a feeling of comfort and elegance to the interior.

BELOW: Compact fluorescent lamps offer remarkable savings in energy costs, giving up to five times more light per watt than filament lamps. They last up to eight times longer, too, and so require infrequent replacement.

Will improving my lighting increase my electricity costs?

Most probably your electricity bill will be considerably reduced! Among many other good ideas, this book tells you about energy-efficient lamps which make wise use of energy. Energy conservation is a matter of national importance. Using energy-efficient lamps can enable you to reduce the amount of electricity you consume, and significantly reduce the long-term cost of your home lighting.

An important development in home lighting is the availability of energy-efficient *compact fluorescent lamps* (CFLs) which are explained in Chapter 11. It is clear that if these versatile and attractive lamps are used to replace those filament lamps in your home that burn for long hours, significant savings in energy costs will result; if, after reading this book, you do no more than go and buy some compact fluorescent lamps to replace just those lamps, you could significantly reduce the amount of electricity that your lighting consumes. CFLs are more costly to buy than filament lamps, but they produce up to five times as much light per watt, and they have an average life of eight times longer, so that, if you operate these lamps for long hours, you will typically make savings (at 1994 values) of £10.00 per annum per energy-saving bulb. The very long life of these lamps makes them particularly suited to

5

locations where it is difficult to get to the lamps, and for lighting in the homes of elderly people who cannot change lamps easily.

If you change from filament lamps to compact fluorescent lamps, and perhaps also install tubular fluorescent lamps in places such as the kitchen, utility room and workshop, the amount of light you obtain may be substantially increased and yet you are likely to reduce your annual lighting cost significantly. Typical savings may be bigger than the cost of VAT on the electricity you use for lighting. Energy-efficient lamps enable you to reduce your outgoings while enjoying the benefits of having more light and more comfortable and elegant lighting in your home. (If you are confused by the references to the various kinds of lamps, see Chapter 11 and the Glossary.)

What does it cost to light a typical home?

Although we may mistakenly refer to the charges for electricity as 'the electric light bill', in fact the bulk of the electricity you buy is consumed by your water heater, space heating, fridge, freezer, cooker, microwave oven, vacuum cleaner, washing machine, tumble dryer, television, hi-fi and other electrical appliances. For an average family of two adults and two children living in a medium-sized semi-detached house, the energy consumed by the lighting is unlikely to exceed 330 kWh (units) per year, which is typically about 9 per cent of the family's total electricity consumption. However, if those filament lamps in your home that operate continuously for long hours of use were to be replaced with compact fluorescent lamps, the annual cost of your lighting would be substantially lower. (See Chapter 11 for more information on compact fluorescent lamps.)

Is it difficult to plan the lighting for one's home?

Not at all. It is a pleasurable and rewarding experience to create attractive lighting for your home. By studying this book, you will be able to decide what sort of lighting fittings and what types of lamps you want to have in your home. The examples of lighting layouts given can be copied for rooms of roughly similar size to give excellent practical results. If the shapes and sizes of the rooms in your house or flat differ greatly from the examples, the ideas can be readily adapted.

Don't be put off by a few unfamiliar words! The terms used are explained generally in the text, but some that you might find mystifying are explained in the Glossary at the back of this book.

Must one know about electrical wiring?

No. If you can wire up a 13 A plug-top, change a fuse and make connections to lampholders, etc., then you should be able to do most of the practical

As explained in Chapter 11, substantial savings in energy cost and in the cost of replacement lamps can easily be achieved by substituting compact fluorescent lamps for those filament lamps in the home which operate for long hours.

things that are described in Part 2. Chapter 9 explains some basic electrical principles, and shows you how to select the correct size of fuse and ensure that you do not overload a circuit.

While most of the ideas described can safely be put into effect by anyone with ordinary DIY knowledge, it is recommended that modifications to the permanent wiring of the house or the installation of an RCD (a protective device – see Chapter 9) should be carried out by a properly qualified electrician.

What is the best way to use this book?

A good plan would be to read through the whole book quickly to make yourself generally familiar with its contents. Then, read Part 1 carefully to see how its recommendations relate to the needs of your home, referring to the Glossary for explanations of any words that are unfamiliar to you, or dipping into Part 2 for more information. At that stage you will probably want to visit one or two lighting shops or your electricity company's showroom, to look at lamps and lighting fittings, and perhaps discuss possible ideas. If you are confused and mystified about modern lamps such as compact fluorescent lamps, read Chapter 11, and then ask your lighting retailer to demonstrate the lamps to you. If you are doubtful about the functions and benefits of the various kinds of lighting fittings, refer to Chapter 3.

Having studied this book, you will be in a better position to make wise choices. When you have decided what improvements you intend to carry out to the lighting of your home, refer to Part 2 for helpful guidelines and methods of installation.

The PRINCIPLES
of good HOME LIGHTING

How can better lighting improve our home environment?

Apart from making the home look more comfortable and welcoming, sufficient and suitable lighting makes all visual tasks easier. For example, it is much easier to read small print or do fine needlework if you have plenty of light on the task. Good lighting helps to prevent eyestrain, and protects the eyesight of the younger members of the family when they are doing their homework or hobbies. Older eyes need more light, too, to help their vision and to prevent accidents – especially on the stairs.

In the kitchen, plentiful light at the sink, at the cooker and on the preparation area is a great boon. Unfortunately, most kitchens have a central ceiling light which ensures that cooks are always standing in their own light – just as they did in those dreadful old Victorian kitchens which were lit by a central gas lamp! In Chapter 4 we look at ways of improving the lighting in your kitchen and getting rid of those annoying shadows.

Tasteful and well-planned lighting in the home makes an important contribution to the decor. Every application of lighting can be individually planned to suit the taste of the occupants, and to accentuate, beautify and harmonise with the room layouts and furnishings.

How does better lighting aid safety?

Good lighting in the kitchen, with the lighting fittings positioned so that the cook does not stand in his or her own light, can help prevent accidents with knives and when moving heavy stewpots. Sufficient light on the stairs and outside the house at the back and front will help to prevent tripping and falling accidents.

What are the benefits of having some outside lights?

Outside lighting at the front of the house will welcome your visitors. It can make the name or number of your house visible, and enable first-time callers

LEFT: Exterior lighting enhances security and safety, and lends a welcoming and attractive appearance to the home.

to find you. It will make your visitors'
approach to your door safer.

An outside light enables you to identify callers before opening the door at
night. If a caller at the front door cannot be seen through a glass panel in the
door, or from a window, an inconspicuous optical spyglass may be fitted to the
door. Some homes, such as apartments
and flats, have a closed-circuit TV camera to enable occupants to identify
callers, and a button which is pressed to
release an electric lock on the street
door. Outside lighting will be needed
for these measures to be effective at
night.

A small amount of outside lighting at
the front, sides and back of your house
will help to make your home safer from
prowlers and burglars. It will also make
it safer at night to go out to the dustbin,
or to the shed or garage.

One or two small floodlight fittings
mounted on the back of the house will
enable your garden or patio to be
enjoyed after dark on summer evenings
– for example, for barbecues or for sitting outside. The floodlighting may
reveal a delightful night view of your
garden as seen from the house – particularly in winter when snow has fallen!

If fitted with modern low-energy
lamps, outdoor lights are economical to run. They can be automatically
operated from dusk to dawn, or arranged to come on only when the presence of a person is detected by a sensing device. See Chapter 8 for more
information on outdoor lighting.

There is a wide choice of functional
and decorative exterior lighting fittings to suit all styles and periods of
houses, so it is easy to blend the
lighting to suit the environment.

What is meant by 'good lighting'?

Good lighting does not necessarily mean having a great quantity of light. It
is the *quality* of the light that largely determines our satisfaction with it. We
are more likely to find our lighting satisfactory if the lighting fittings are not
glaring, i.e. not so uncomfortably bright that we cannot look at them directly.

Although we may use strongly directional spotlights and accent lighting for drama and interest, the general lighting of a room should provide a soft spread of light over the whole room, without any part of it being deeply shadowed.

To say that we have 'good lighting' means that we have chosen suitable lamps and lighting fittings to give us the quality and quantity of light we need for the particular room. It may also mean that the lighting can be readily adjusted to suit different uses of the room at different times of day. We are concerned with the safety and the appearance of the lighting fittings, and their cost. We are concerned with the cost of the energy consumed by the lamps and the cost of periodically replacing them, although convenience and elegance are also important.

What is glare?

Glare is the discomfort that we experience when part of our visual field is excessively bright compared with the brightness to which our eyes are adapted. Sometimes people experiencing glare may complain that 'there is too much light'; but glare is not caused by this. One is more likely to suffer glare in a room that has a poor lighting level.

Rarely, you may suffer 'disabling glare' which prevents you from seeing what you want to see – for example, glare from the bright headlights of an oncoming car on a dark road at night. More commonly we experience 'discomfort glare', which may be tiring and irritating, but which does not prevent us from seeing. Glare may be 'direct' or 'indirect'. An example of direct glare is that caused by looking at a bare lamp or an overbright lighting fitting, particularly if seen against a dark background. We suffer indirect glare when we see the image of a bare lamp or a bright lighting fitting reflected from a glossy surface, such as a polished tabletop (see Chapter 10).

A room in which the lighting is uniform and virtually glare-free will be a bland, boring sort of interior. For visual interest, we need some bright spots, and possibly some directional lighting to give a focus of attention.

In a domestic room, carefully controlled contrasts of brightness can be very artistic. Remember that you are not trying to produce a totally glare-free environment. Moderate contrasts of brightness in a room, and even a little glare, are quite acceptable.

How can a room be well lit without creating uncomfortable glare?

There is an almost infinite number of ways in which any particular room can be lit. To reduce direct glare, the first requirement is usually to place shades or reflectors around the lamps so that their brightness is shielded from normal view. Selecting lampshades for the portable and fixed lights in the

room gives great scope for individual taste and imagination, by choice of their size, shape, material and colour.

With the exception of some candle lamps, bare lamps are generally unacceptable. Most lamps, including fluorescent tubes – and even compact fluorescent lamps – are too bright to be looked at directly. In small rooms – a small kitchen, say – bare fluorescent tubes at ceiling level might be tolerable if well away from the normal angles of view (but putting them in diffusing fittings would be much better).

Whether in a mansion or a cottage, lighting can be a dominant feature of the interior decor.

Because glare is caused by excessive contrast in brightness, a lighting fitting may be uncomfortably glaring when seen against dark furnishings, yet tolerable if seen against a light-coloured surface. Changing the lamps to others of lesser power will not reduce the glare very much, but will reduce the amount of light available for seeing. With care in choosing the lighting fittings and in positioning them – as well as in choosing the room colours – it is possible to provide all the light that is needed for tasks and for good appearance of the room without causing any noticeable discomfort from glare.

How might one introduce changes in the lighting to suit the time of day and the occasion?

Our need for lighting in any room is not constant. During the day we may use electric lighting to augment the light that enters through the window. As daylight fades, we may want to put on some more lights for comfort. After dark, our use of a room – a sitting room, say – may change several times during an evening, when the children are doing homework, having dinner, or watching television. Each activity may justify making adjustment to the lighting.

Adjusting the lighting to our needs of the moment can be no more difficult than simply switching the overhead lights off, or switching on a standard-lamp or an uplighter. We may have a combination of uses of the room; for example, while one person is watching television (and needs to have the general lighting subdued), another member of the family may be sitting in an armchair reading or doing some needlework (and need to use a local shaded lamp or spotlight). Spotlights may be free standing, or mobile devices on their own floor stands, or may be permanently installed on track, or surface mounted or recessed into the ceiling.

Another important way in which we can introduce interesting and attractive changes in the lighting scene is by the use of dimmers (see Chapter 13). Dimmers can be used to great effect in the living room where dramatic changes of mood can be created by touching the dimmer control. Dimmers are a great boon in bedrooms too, especially in the bedrooms of small children.

A neat, portable reading-lamp will provide plenty of light for reading or sewing etc and prevent eyestrain, without the need to brighten the whole room.

How does lighting affect our perception of colour?

It is possible to distinguish between the 'colour appearance' of a lamp and its 'colour rendering'. *Colour appearance* is the appearance of the lamp itself or of a white object seen in its light. We describe a lamp of bluish appearance as 'cold', and one of a pinkish appearance as 'warm'. Our judgement of colour appearance may be confused by the phenomenon of 'colour adaptation', by which we tend to adapt to any non-white colour of light and cease to be conscious of its non-whiteness.

Colour rendering is the ability of the light from a lamp to render faithfully colours other than white. It is possible to match two colours under the light of a particular type of lamp, and then to discover that, when viewed under different lighting, the two colours are not identical. A true colour match is one that holds good under all lighting conditions.

Contrary to popular belief, matching colours under natural light from the sky does not necessarily produce the best results. Daylight is not constant, but varies in its colour composition from minute to minute. Taking a garment to the door of the shop to see it by daylight is not a reliable way of judging its colour. If there is any benefit in taking the object to see it in daylight, it is mainly because the daylight is brighter. A key factor in seeing colour well is to have plenty of light.

Although the light from ordinary filament lamps and 'Warm White' fluorescent tubes is weak in blue content, most people find their colour rendering reasonably satisfactory provided that the light on the task is plentiful. The use of 'colour matching' or 'artificial daylight' fluorescent tubular lamps to light home tasks involving colour discrimination is hardly ever justified. The light from *tungsten-halogen lamps* (see Chapter 11) is richer in blue than that from filament lamps, and therefore is of somewhat better colour rendering. For typical tasks involving colour judgement at home, such as embroidery and stamp collecting, the light from a reading lamp or spotlamp containing a tungsten-halogen lamp will give adequate revealment of colour provided that the lamp is brought near to the task so that it receives plenty of light.

What is the effect of strongly coloured decor?

In home lighting installations, quite a large proportion of the light from the lamps is reflected one or more times from the room surfaces before it is finally 'utilised' by arriving on the tabletop or other surface that we wish to light. White light is actually a mixture of all the colours of the rainbow; when light is reflected from a coloured surface, its colour is changed by selective reflection and absorption of the various colours of which it is composed, so it finally takes on a composition determined at least in part by the colours in the room. This effect can be quite unpleasant – for example, if there is considerable reflection of light from strongly coloured room surfaces in the dining room (especially from green or blue walls), it will tend to make meat on the plate look dark, brownish and quite unappetising, and fruit will look lacklustre.

In Chapter 3 we discuss the value of having a dining-table lamp mounted low over the table so that its light comes directly to the food without reflec-

A table lamp with a translucent shade throws a soft diffused light around the room, providing a subtle flow of light.

tions from the room surfaces. This ensures that the light from it is of pure colour, with the result that the food on the table will look as fresh and attractive as it really is.

How might one design the lighting and colour scheme for a room?

If the walls, carpeting and furnishings are of strong colours, the light reflected from them will take on a tinge of the dominant colour. Things are simpler if only pale colours are used for the decor, e.g. white, cream, very pale eau-de-nil, very pale greys, magnolia, etc. These will not greatly change the colour of light reflected from them. However, to avoid creating a wishy-washy, colourless interior or lending a white, clinical and impersonal appearance to the rooms, one may add colour in small areas, for example, by introducing brightly coloured objects, or perhaps lighting a small area or object with a spotlight fitted with a coloured lamp or colour filter.

A single strongly coloured object, a fine vase or picture, say – preferably not too big – can be selectively illuminated to create an interesting focal centre. Coloured spotlights, ceiling mounted or on lighting track, can create dramatic interest by illuminating small areas of a pale wall or ceiling with a splash of vivid colour.

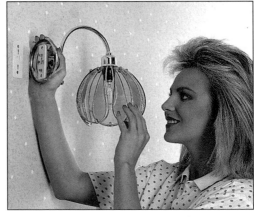

'Plug-in' ceiling roses and wall-bracket connectors enable easy removal of lighting fittings for cleaning, to exchange them for others, or when decorating the room.

How might one introduce changes in the decor and lighting from time to time?

Using a neutral decor, and adding colour as described, makes it easier to bring about refreshing changes in the appearance of your room from time to time. For example, pictures or coloured objects of decor can be moved or exchanged for others; the portable lighting fittings can be moved or changed, and adjustable spotlights might be turned in new directions to

Unplugging a lighting fitting or restoring it can be done safely in seconds without tools, and without having to interfere with the electrical connections.

highlight different features. Such changes can be made easily and without expense.

You will gain in flexibility if your rooms have plenty of socket outlets, so that you may position portable lighting fittings in any room wherever your fancy takes you.

'Plug-in' ceiling roses and wall-light connectors can be fitted to your existing points. These enable lighting fittings to be easily taken down at any time for cleaning, and restored instantly, without any interference with the electrical wiring. Once these devices are in place, in a matter of moments it is possible to exchange the lighting fittings between rooms or to put up a different lighting fitting to suit a special occasion. If you are moving into a new house, or having your house rewired, take the opportunity to install plug-in ceiling rose devices for all ceiling points and for your wall-light points too.

Why should lighting levels be increased for the elderly?

Most of us discover in time that from about the age of 40 we need rather more light to see well. As we age, our eyes need greater illuminance (quantity of light) on our tasks in order to see well. This fact explains why many elderly people have considerable difficulty in reading small print or threading needles. And, because elderly people cannot see so well in subdued light, they are in greater danger of tripping over objects on the floor (especially if they are wearing bifocal spectacles), or of falling down poorly lit stairs. The visual needs of most elderly people can be readily satisfied by following the guidelines given in this book. Remember that older people may be more susceptible to glare than younger folk, so any increase of illuminance must be accompanied by rather less glare than might be tolerable in a home occupied only by younger persons.

What are the special lighting needs of persons with a visual handicap?

The lighting needs of partially sighted people or persons with some degree of visual handicap depend on the nature and the severity of their particular visual disability. Generally, they benefit from the provision of plentiful lighting with minimum glare, as do elderly people.

For both elderly and partially sighted people, safety in the home can be improved by suitable lighting. A useful expedient is to paint things in contrasting colours so that they can be seen more readily. Lights can be positioned so as to enhance vision; even shadows from carefully arranged lighting can help revealment (as in lighting stairs, discussed in Chapter 6).

Helpful advice for people with visual problems is obtainable from the Partially Sighted Society. For example, in addition to a good level of general lighting and the restriction of glare, the visually handicapped person might need an illuminated reading magnifier, which is a magnifying lens large enough to cover a page of a book, and which incorporates one or two small lamps so that the page is very well illuminated without any direct glare and without any distracting reflections from the paper.

What special opportunities to improve the lighting occur when one is redecorating a room?

Redecorating gives one the chance to make changes to the lighting that would not be possible at other times. For example, you might decide to dispense with an existing ceiling point, or move it to a new position, or install some extra ceiling points, or install a run of lighting track, which will give you the opportunity to ring the changes to your lighting in the years to come.

When a room is in normal use, it may not be possible to consider installing wall-mounted lighting fittings, because the cabling must be concealed in the wall for neatness. But, if the walls are going to be stripped anyway, this is the golden opportunity to get this job done. The channels cut in the wall for the wiring can be neatly plastered over, and will be quite invisible when the room is re-papered.

Look at the various ideas described in Chapter 14, and see if any of them could be utilised in your home. For example, if you have a high-ceilinged room, you might consider installing a lighting cove. Or, if you are thinking of putting up new curtains, consider having lighting pelmets installed over the windows (and remember to buy a little extra material for this purpose).

Finally, remember that redecorating is the time for installing some extra socket outlets. You really can't have too many!

What are the possibilities of introducing lighting into the garden?

Earlier in this chapter we discussed outdoor lighting intended for the essential purposes of safety and security. Consider now how you might install some lighting in your garden purely for pleasure. Of course, if your garden is illuminated, you might be able to do odd jobs out there after dark (and perhaps use your garden swimming pool if you have one). The main benefits of garden lighting are spectacle and enjoyment.

In Chapter 8 we review ideas such as floodlighting the garden so that you can sit out on warm evenings or perhaps have a barbecue after dark. Then there are the pleasures of seeing your garden lit with 'spike lamps' for a special occasion. For a summer garden party you might put up lengths of festoon lighting, with coloured bulbs to give a really jolly and festive appearance. Later in the year you could use the same festoon lighting to illuminate an outdoor Christmas tree.

Lighting enables the garden to be enjoyed at night. Many interesting and colourful effects can be produced.

In Chapter 15 we discuss ways of installing garden lighting. You will probably need some help from a properly qualified electrician to install one or two outdoor socket outlets (and the electrical protection of them), but, once they are in place, all sorts of delightful possibilities become practicable.

If the windows of your home look out over the garden, you will have the pleasure of seeing your garden literally in a new light. When entertaining guests, it can be really impressive to dim down the room lights, and draw back the curtains so that they can enjoy the spectacle of your garden lit up for the occasion.

Will fibre-optics become an important part of home lighting in the future?

Many people think so, for exciting new lighting ideas can now be realised by the use of *fibre-optic lightguides*. These enable light to be 'piped' considerable distances from the lamp to the point of use, and the fibres can be bent to almost any configuration. The fibres may be 'dark' (i.e. they conduct all the light to a distant point where it emerges from a small lighting fitting), or 'luminous' (i.e. they radiate light along their length). The fibres can handle coloured light as well as ordinary white light.

It has been visualised that one day we will have just one or two large, very efficient lamps, perhaps tucked away in the attic, and from these lamps fibre-optic lightguides will conduct light to every part of the house. Because fibre-optic fibres do not heat up, and contain no electricity, they are entirely free from all risks of fire or electric shock.

Fibre-optic light distribution systems are now being used to a limited extent in commerce and industry, but the technology is still in its infancy. At the time of writing, fibre-optics have only penetrated home lighting in very minor ways; for example, in the form of decorative lamps with glowing optical fibres. But Emma Dawson-Tarr, managing director of Absolute Action Ltd, specialists in fibre-optic lighting, is one of the visionary engineers who sees a great future for this technology. She predicts that, within a few years, fibre-optic light distribution systems will be installed routinely in new dwellings, and will result in very efficient use of energy and extremely low running costs, as well as opening up attractive new ways of lighting our homes.

What is emergency lighting, and where is it necessary?

Emergency lighting is battery-powered lighting that comes into operation automatically on failure of the normal electrical supply, and provides sufficient light to enable people to escape during a fire or other emergency when the normal lighting is not functioning. Emergency lighting is a legal

There are self-contained emergency lights which light up if the mains electricity fails, and automatically recharge themselves after use, yet look just like ordinary lighting fittings.

requirement in hotels, boarding houses, residential institutions and on some common stairs and entrances in multiple-occupancy premises and blocks of flats. There is no legal obligation to install emergency lighting in ordinary homes, but if you let rooms in your house, you may be required by law to install both emergency lighting and smoke detectors or fire alarms – your local authority or fire prevention officer will be able to advise you on this. The current Building Regulations require smoke detectors to be fitted in all new dwellings and in major extensions to dwellings.

Even though there may be no legal obligation to install it, emergency lighting could be a lifesaver in a large house with difficult stairs, particularly if there are older people in the family, or if the bedrooms are on several floors. Seek the advice of the fire prevention officer on this. Modern emergency lighting fittings are of such pleasing appearance that they are quite inconspicuous and can be mistaken for ordinary lighting fittings.

Lighting for
the **LIVING ROOM**

The types of lamps mentioned in this and the following chapters are described in Chapter 11. Advice regarding buying the types of lighting fittings mentioned in this and the following chapters is given in Chapter 12. More information about dimming will be found in Chapter 13.

How may 'general lighting' be arranged?

General lighting is the provision of a moderate level of lighting for the whole room for comfort and safe movement. Such lighting was traditionally provided by a central pendant fitting (Figure 3.1). In modern homes an attractive general spread of light might be provided by low-glare sources such as ceiling-recessed downlighters which conceal the lamp from view (Figure 3.2). General lighting can also be obtained from free-standing uplighters (Figure 3.3), from open-topped standard lamps (Figure 3.4), or from wall-mounted fittings which project part of their light upward (Figure 3.5). A gentle flow of light onto the ceiling and upper walls gives the room a relaxed, comfortable feeling.

A subdued and pleasant form of general lighting is created by installing small floodlights which are termed 'wall-washers' (Figure 3.6). These are aimed to bounce their light off one or more walls to spread light diffusely across the room. Wall-washers are usually ceiling mounted (individually, or on lighting track) or ceiling recessed, or can be mounted at the head or foot of the wall. Wall-washing can be an important feature of your decor.

The general lighting should be augmented as required by portable units such as table lamps, floor standards and reading lamps (Figure 3.4). Spill light and reflected light from spotlights (Figure 3.7) and other lighting features such as cove lighting (Figure 3.8) whose function is mainly decorative, will also contribute to the level of general lighting.

An interesting effect can be produced by the use of *picture lights*. These are small wall-mounted lighting fittings containing a linear lamp (e.g. an architectural tubular lamp or a small fluorescent tubular lamp) mounted on

FIGURE 3.1 CENTRAL PENDANT LIGHTING FITTING.
The most common form of room lighting. Centre pendants tend to produce direct glare if overbright. They may produce a rather uninteresting distribution of light by themselves, and need to be augmented by other lighting in the room.

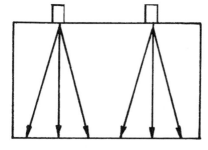

FIGURE 3.2 DOWNLIGHTERS.
Downlighters offer an attractive way of providing general lighting in a living room without dominating the scene as pendant fittings tend to do. As the name suggests, downlighters direct their light downward and therefore do not provide much light on the ceiling or the vertical surfaces of the room, so that some other lighting will probably also be required.

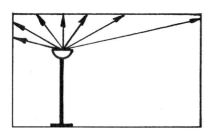

FIGURE 3.3 UPLIGHTING.
The general lighting of a room can be provided by one or possibly two uplighters which give upward light only, the light being reflected from the ceiling and upper walls to produce a gentle flow of light over the whole room.

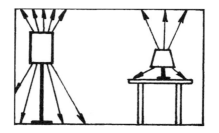

FIGURE 3.4 PORTABLE LIGHTING.
Floor-mounted standard lamps, pedestal lamps and table lamps of various kinds can be placed where light is needed or for decorative effect.

FIGURE 3.5 WALL-BRACKET FITTINGS.
These may provide most of the general lighting, or may be employed mainly for their pleasant effect and appearance.

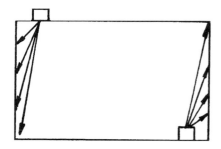

FIGURE 3.6 WALL-WASHERS.
Wall-washers can provide a striking lighting feature when used to illuminate pictures, curtains or displays of plants. The soft reflected light may be quite sufficient for movement about the room and for watching TV.

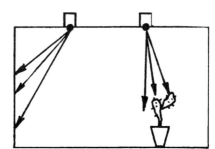

FIGURE 3.7 SPOTLIGHTS.
Individual spotlights, or clusters of spotlights, ceiling mounted or mounted on lighting track, enable features in the room to be given an attractive emphasis.

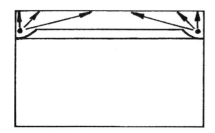

FIGURE 3.8 COVE OR CORNICE LIGHTING.
An existing architectural cove may be utilised, or runs of cornice lighting fittings installed, to give soft lighting to the room reflected from the ceiling and upper walls, the lamps being completely concealed.

a wall bracket, and designed to cast light downward to illuminate a picture while shielding the lamp from normal angles of view. If several of these are used, the spill-light will produce a very subdued but pleasant flow of light about the room while directing attention to the pictures.

What are the functions of 'downlights' and 'spotlights'?

Downlights are ceiling-mounted or ceiling-recessed lighting fittings having the function, as the name suggests, to direct light downward. They provide good 'cut-off ' (i.e. they shield the lamp so that it cannot be seen from normal angles of view) and are therefore inconspicuous, yet they make a good contribution to the general lighting. The only time that downlights are intrusive is perhaps when we lie back on the settee and look upward! A room lit only with downlights would result in the ceiling being in comparative darkness, so it would be advisable to have some other fittings in the room which give an upward flow of light.

Spotlights also may be ceiling-mounted or ceiling recessed, or may be mounted on lighting track. They may be 'eyeball' type or have swivelled reflectors. They provide emphasis, not general lighting. They direct light at a required angle, providing interest and drama by highlighting objects or parts of walls. Those containing a 'reflector spotlamp' (a type of filament lamp in a blown-glass reflector bulb) give a fairly widespread soft-edged bright patch. Those containing an 'LVTH lamp' (a miniature, low-voltage tungsten-halogen dichroic reflector lamp) produce a small, well-defined bright patch of light. The latter are more cost-

ABOVE: When pictures are lit, they literally come out of the shadows to become centres of interest, and the spill-light contributes gently to the general lighting of the room.

FAR LEFT: Recessed downlights can provide excellent general lighting, while being inconspicuous in use. They are hardly noticeable during the day.

LEFT: Recessed 'eyeball' spotlights can be aimed to give attractive emphasis lighting of objects, or to provide adequate light for reading etc without glare.

RIGHT: A combination of downlights and spotlights enables a room to be lit without the use of table lamps or floor-standing lamps.

ly to install, but are more economical to operate than blown-glass spotlights. An attractive arrangement is to have a cluster of three or more LVTH adjustable spotlights mounted on ceiling track.

What are the functions of fixed lighting features and portable lighting?

Fixed lighting features are those that are permanently installed and connected directly to the house wiring system. The fixed lighting features in a room tend to determine the room's general appearance. By switching or by operating a dimmer control, such lighting can be adjusted to produce the quantity and quality of light to suit the needs of the moment.

Lighting fittings such as table lamps, reading lamps, floor standards, etc., the leads of which are plugged into socket outlets, are portable lighting fit-

In a room with adequate general lighting, elegant table lamps can provide visual interest even if their contribution to the illumination of the room is limited.

tings which may be placed where desired, either for decorative effect or to provide enhanced light on a task. They are easy to move to different positions in the room from time to time. Indeed, such fittings may occasionally be exchanged with those from other rooms in the house to create a fresh appearance.

Uplighters will provide general lighting over a large area of a room – or even the whole of it – by their light which is reflected from the ceiling and upper walls. Free-standing uplighters are 'portable' in that they could be moved to a different position in the room without much trouble, but users tend to find a convenient position for them, and leave them there all the time.

What is the value of dimming controls for lighting?

Although dimming is still regarded by some as a luxury feature, the facility to have a graduated control of illuminance is a valuable refinement of the lighting in a living room. Dimmers are also of particular value in bedrooms (see Chapter 5).

In a room where one watches television or operates a home computer, dimming of the overhead light – or of all the lights in the room – will enhance viewing comfort. Lowering the ambient lighting level means that you can reduce the brightness of the TV screen and thus get a better picture (and probably also extend the life of the cathode-ray tube). When one is showing home videos, dimming the 'house lights' as the titles come up on the screen lends an air of professionalism to the show.

There is a touch of luxury in being able to dim down the room lights and allow the dining light over the table to provide most of the light for eating.

You will find more information about dimming in Chapter 13.

How might one light a dining area or dining room?

The key to effective lighting for dining is flexibility. All the ideas for lounges and sitting rooms discussed in this chapter are appropriate to a dining room. Additional lighting for the dining table may also be required.

It should be remembered that meals taken at the table differ very greatly according to the occasion and who is present. For a jolly family meal with young people or children present, quite bright lights are appropriate; for example, the dining-table light might be used, and all the room lights left on.

For a child's birthday party (when the candles on the cake will be seen burning brightly if the room lighting is subdued), or for a romantic dinner for two (when large candles – real wax ones, or some of those almost-convincing electric ones – are used to shed a soft, intimate light), the general

lighting should be turned right down. By dimming or switching off the general lighting, the table can be made the centre of attention and dominate the scene. In Chapter 1 we mentioned the value of installing a dining-table light in rooms with strongly coloured decor. A dining-table lamp swamps out the light that is reflected from the coloured surfaces in the room, and it really makes the food on the table look better!

A light over the dining table increases the social pleasure of the meal, and enhances the appearance of the food, but should not be over-bright as seen by the diners.

A dining-table light can be fitted with a 'raising and lowering' device so that it can be lowered to give a strong illumination on the table (but not so low that it prevents the diners seeing each other!). The device also enables the dining-table light to be raised out of the way if the table is moved for any reason, e.g. when having a party.

ABOVE RIGHT: Because the light from a dining table lamp flows directly to the table and is not affected by the colours of the room, it can reveal the colours of food attractively.

Is there scope for some imaginative thinking regarding lighting for the home?

There certainly is! Think of lighting as a means of decor as well as a utilitarian service. And remember that there are two aspects of the decorative effects of lighting – the appearance of the lighting fittings themselves, and the effects of light and shade that are produced.

With quite moderate expenditure, some interesting effects can be achieved. Let us quote two examples. The first concerns a family who wanted to have a pin-up board where the children could display their drawings. They purchased a cork-faced board measuring about 600 mm x 800 mm, and then found that the only clear area of wall they had where it could possibly be fixed was in the living room, where the new board looked rather dominating and not particularly charming. They then had a bright idea and, instead of fixing the board directly to the wall, they mounted it on four wooden blocks, so that the back of the board was about 50 mm clear of the wall. Behind the pin-up board they fixed a 15 W fluorescent tubular lamp fitting (450 mm long), which, while the lamp itself was completely concealed, gave an interesting 'halo' flow of light on the adjacent wall. This turned the pin-up board into a novel and attractive feature, the lamp giving a gentle glare-free glow of light over the whole room when the other room lights were subdued.

Another interesting innovation concerned the family that returned from a holiday in Italy with a really charming and colourful piece of stained glass which measured about 300 mm wide by 500 mm high. They hung it inside the lounge window on two thin wires, where it looked very attractive during the day, but at night its colourful effect was lost. This they corrected by

LEFT: Recessed downlights are inconspicuous and do not clutter the scene, imparting a feeling of spaciousness to the room.

RIGHT: If direct glare is well controlled, contrasts in brightness and in quality of light flowing within a room can be most attractive.

installing a small external lighting fitting in the garden, which gave some attractive lighting at the back of the house at night, shed sufficient light for walking along the garden path safely, and also back-illuminated the stained-glass panel so that, seen from within the living room, its beautiful colours glowed most attractively. Further, when the other lights in the lounge were

An alcove or recess can be transformed into an interesting feature by introducing lighting, whether enclosed by a glass door or with open shelving (see Page 114).

dimmed, the little floodlight outside, shining through the stained glass, cast interesting patches of coloured light onto the ceiling.

If you have a wall recess or an alcove (for example, beside a fireplace) you could turn it into a really attractive feature by installing 'alcove lighting'. Concealed lighting from a pelmet light above, perhaps with additional lights at the edges of shelves, will enable you to display your collection of interesting treasures such as pottery, glass, miniature models or framed photographs. The shelves may be of glass to let the light through, or solid shelves could be used with lamps concealed under them. Some basic ways of creating alcove lighting are described in Chapter 14 and shown in Figure 14.11, but the general theme could be interpreted to suit your preferences.

Lighting for *the* KITCHEN

What are the problems in lighting kitchens?

The kitchen is the hub of life in the home. It is the creative workshop where food is prepared, and is the room in which the housewife or househusband spends a great deal of time. In many homes, the kitchen is also the breakfast room or dining room.

Generally, lighting in kitchens is a problem area. While owner-occupiers may be willing to invest in the cost of extra lighting points, occupiers of rented properties may be reluctant to pay for modifications to the house wiring or for built-in improvements. However, some of the suggestions made in this chapter do not involve any change to the permanent wiring of the house.

Surveys have indicated that 90 per cent of kitchens are poorly lit, many having only a single ceiling lighting fitting containing a filament lamp. This results in one's shadow being cast onto the task when working at the sink, at the cooker, or at the worktops (see Figure 4.1). Things may be slightly better if the important work positions are all along walls parallel to a central long

FIGURE 4.1
In this and the following diagrams, P represents a person standing at a task, S is the sink, C the cooker, and L a lighting fitting. The dot-hatched areas are those in shadow.

Nothing is more tiring and irritating than trying to work when you are 'standing in your own light'. In this typical kitchen lighting scheme with only a single central lighting fitting, anyone working at the sink, at the cooker or at the worktops will work in the shadow cast by their body.

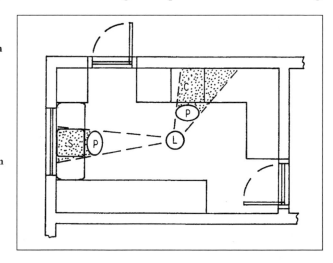

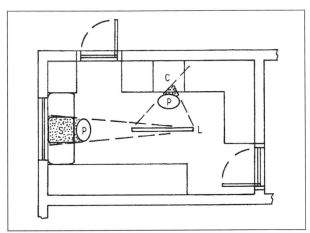

FIGURE 4.2
Replacing the central lighting fitting with one containing a long fluorescent tubular lamp can improve the lighting on only one axis. A work-position end-on to the fitting will still tend to be shadowed by the person standing at it, although having a white ceiling and upper walls will help to reflect the light and spread it more evenly.

fluorescent tubular lamp fitting, but if, as is usual, work positions are on two walls, one of them will be deeply shadowed (see Figure 4.2).

What are the requirements for general lighting in a typical domestic kitchen?

A white matt ceiling and light-coloured upper walls will make any lighting system more effective by reflecting light and spreading it more evenly. The lighting in any kitchen or kitchen-diner will be significantly improved if the single central fitting is replaced by at least two ceiling-mounted lighting fittings spaced widely apart so that light flows to the tasks on either side of a person standing at a work position (see Figure 4.3). In a small or medium-sized room (up to about 2 m x 3.5 m), use at least two lighting fittings with opal enclosures of about 250 mm diameter, each containing lamps emitting a total

A kitchen which serves as the breakfast room or dining room needs flexible lighting to provide the right visual conditions for cooking and for dining.

35

Lighting in the kitchen must be adaptable to cheer up grey winter mornings as well as providing a comfortable light to work under.

FIGURE 4.3
The lighting can be improved by having at least two ceiling-mounted lighting fittings, strategically placed so as to minimise shadowing. Four or more would be better! One method might be to mount directable spotlamps along a length of ceiling-mounted lighting track.

FIGURE 4.4
If fluorescent lighting is preferred, use at least two 'bare-batten' or (preferably) enclosed diffusing fittings, each containing one or two 36 W 1,200 mm fluorescent tubes.

of 1,300 to 1,400 lumens, e.g. each containing one 100 W filament lamp, or two 60 W filament lamps, or one 23 W Type PL electronic compact fluorescent lamp etc. See Figure 11.5 in Chapter 11 for comparisons of the light outputs of the various types of compact fluorescent lamps.

In a kitchen with light-coloured walls and ceiling, two ceiling-mounted diffusing lighting fittings, each housing a 36 W 1,200 mm tubular fluores-

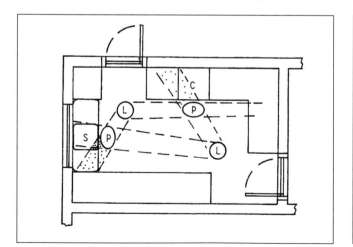

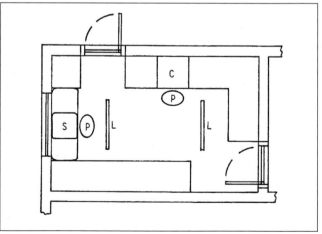

LIGHTING FOR THE KITCHEN

A kitchen-diner needs plenty of light for the cook's work without annoying shadows on the task, but the lighting must look sociable. The ability to switch the lights individually is very desirable.

cent lamp, can be used without creating too much glare. Light from these long lamps will flow past on either side of the person working and thus give little shadowing, while the reflection of light from the upper walls and ceiling will even out the illumination (see Figure 4.4) and tend to reduce direct glare.

A neat and convenient way of deploying a group of lighting fittings on the ceiling is to mount them on one or more lengths of lighting track. This has the advantage that only one electrical connection has to be made to each length of track.

With any system of general lighting in a kitchen, some 'local lighting' will probably also be required.

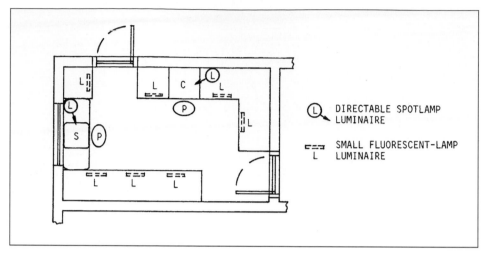

L   DIRECTABLE SPOTLAMP
     LUMINAIRE

L   SMALL FLUORESCENT-LAMP
     LUMINAIRE

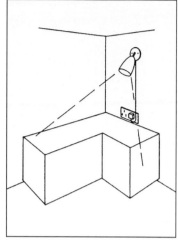

How can 'local lighting' improve the lighting of kitchen worktops?

Local lighting can provide much higher illuminances on the point of work than can be achieved with general lighting only. If a cooker hood is fitted, it will incorporate lighting to illuminate the hob. For lighting at the sink and other work positions, good results can be obtained by installing one or more directable spotlamp fittings, each containing a 60 W mushroom reflector lamp (or a compact fluorescent lamp of similar lumen output) as shown in Figure 4.5. The reflector should conceal the lamp from view (Figure 4.6).

These days, offers of built-in kitchens generally include lighting under the wall cabinets. If you are installing your own wall cabinets, or upgrading an old kitchen, you may wish to install under-cabinet lighting. Small 'bare-batten' fittings, each containing one 8 W 'Warm White' 15 mm diameter x 290 mm long fluorescent tubular lamp (complete with switch), may be positioned on the underside of wall-mounted cupboard units to throw light onto worktops (see Figure 4.5). If there is no recess under the cupboard units to conceal the lamps from view, it is not too difficult a DIY job to fit a wooden pelmet at the front edge of the cupboard base as shown in Figure 4.7.

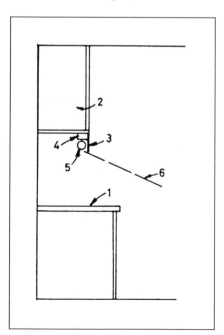

FIGURE 4.5
This sketch indicates the use of directable spotlamp fittings, and of small fluorescent-lamp batten fittings mounted on the underside of wall cabinets.

FIGURE 4.6
Wall-mounted or ceiling-mounted directable spotlamp fittings enable light to be directed exactly to where it is needed.

FIGURE 4.7
Good lighting can be provided on a kitchen worktop (1) by mounting small linear lamp fittings on the underside of wall cabinets (2). If there is no recess under the base, the lamps can be concealed by providing a wooden pelmet (3). If necessary, a wooden batten (4) may be used to position the lamps, which could be 8 W 290 mm long fluorescent tubular lamp batten fittings (5), or linear architectural lamps which do not need ballasts could be employed. The lamp position should be such that the cut-off angle (6) extends well beyond the front of the worktop (1).

RIGHT: Specific lighting for specific tasks in the kitchen makes the work easier, as well as being vital for safety and enabling all surfaces to be kept spotlessly clean.

If it is desired not to modify the permanent wiring, local lighting fittings can be fed from a nearby socket outlet. The wiring from socket outlets to these fittings can be concealed and protected by running it in surface-mounted *mini-trunking* as explained in Chapter 14. The lighting fittings should be properly earthed, and a fuse of the correct rating used in the plug-top. Fuse ratings are explained in Chapter 9.

An excellent way of providing a good standard of lighting at a sink that is positioned in front of a window is to install a *pelmet light* as described in Chapter 14.

LEFT: Under-canopy lighting puts the light where the cook needs it, right on the task.

ABOVE: Localising the lighting to the important working positions in the kitchen removes the annoyance of standing in one's own light.

Lighting for BEDROOMS *and* BATHROOMS

BEDROOMS

What are the principles for lighting a bedroom for adults?

In decorating and lighting bedrooms, personal taste is likely to prevail over technicalities. High intensities of lighting are not needed, for there are no 'visual tasks', apart perhaps from reading in bed and the need to have really good lighting at the dressing table mirror.

Many modern bedrooms have no general lighting, i.e. there is no lighting point in the middle of the ceiling, and reliance is placed on light spilling from bed lights, with wall lights and mirror lights providing the moderate amount of illumination needed for moving about the room.

If any general lighting is provided, this should certainly be very soft and subdued in character, and is probably best derived from well-shaded wall lights in which the lamps are completely screened from view and cast their light mainly upwards. Such gentle lighting may be of particular value during a time of sickness, when the room is occupied for longer hours.

What are the considerations regarding lighting and colour of decor in bedrooms?

We all tend to associate certain colours with particular moods and occasions, and this

Bedside lights which are pleasing to look at and harmonious with the decor will help to create a peaceful bedroom ambiance.

Choose a bedside lamp which will not easily tip over, and place an inconspicuous disk of high-friction plastic sheet under it to prevent it slipping off the bedside table.

For reading in bed, a tall bedside lamp is better. By use of a dimmer, the lamp can be turned down to just a comforting glow which will not disturb the sleeper.

seems to operate strongly when we are choosing the decor for bedrooms. Associations between colour and mood are highly personal but, typically, blue decor is held to be cool and calm, green or yellow decor is felt to be appropriate for a child's or young person's room, while pale pinkish tones of decor are associated with romance, warmth, gentleness and repose.

By the use of suitable lighting, the mood colour of the room can be changed for day and for night occupation. For example, consider a bedroom that is decorated in white or a very pale tint of apple green. By day the room would have a calm, cool appearance, but at night, switching on pink, warm-coloured lighting would tend to make it take on an entirely different cosy night-time appearance. The coloration of the light is readily achieved by the use of pink colour-sprayed lamps in wall lights or overhead lighting fittings. Further, the bedside lamps could use ordinary opal-bulb filament lamps in translucent shades which are white inside and a warm colour on the outside, so that the shades take on a pleasant warm glow when the lamp is lit.

FIGURE 5.1
Bedhead lighting. Tall, well-shaded bedside table lamps permit one person to read in bed while the other sleeps. An in-line dimmer may be fitted in the lead to each fitting, or dimmer devices may be located in the lamp bases.

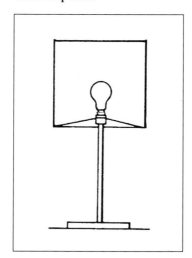

How may bedhead lighting be arranged for a twin-bedded or double-bedded room?

Individual bedhead lights fixed to the wall or attached to tall headboards may be suitable for a single-bedded room. But, for two persons sleeping in a double bed or in twin beds placed close together, unless the lamps are very well shaded they may be overbright, so that the light used by one person for reading in bed will disturb the other.

If there is a bedside cabinet between two beds, two adjustable reading lamps may be used, directed so that one pillow area is illuminated while the other remains in relative darkness. The lamps should be separately switched and – preferably – each fitted with a dimmer.

A good solution to the bedhead lighting problem for twin beds or a double bed is to use two bedside cabinets to support suitable shaded table lamps. The cabinets should be placed on the outer sides of the two beds. The height of bedside cabinets is usually about the same as the height to the top of the mattress, so ordinary squat table lamps (such as are used in living rooms) will not be suitable. One must shop around to find a pattern of table lamp with a stem that is tall enough to enable the lamp to shed light from its large open-bottom shade onto one's book when reading in bed (see Figure 5.1). A cylindrically shaped shade which provides upward and downward light – but which spreads little or no light horizontally – will be suitable.

Are there any risks in using certain types of bedhead lighting?

Caution is advised in purchasing certain patterns of bedhead lamps that clip to the top of the bedhead board. Cases have occurred where such units have become detached, and the hot lamp has burnt the occupant of the bed or has set the bed on fire.

Switching bedside lamps by means of a switch fitted in the lampholder is not recommended, for a sleepy person can easily burn their fingers on the hot filament lamp (although compact fluorescent lamps are much cooler!). Wall-mounted bedhcad lights should have easily reached pendant 'pear' switches. If a bedside lamp does not have a switch on its pedestal, a 'torpedo' switch may be fitted in its supply lead where it can be easily reached from the bed.

There would be danger of electric shock and of sustaining cuts if a bedside table lamp were to fall off the bedside cabinet and the bulb smashed. Therefore, bedside table lamps should have heavy bases so that they will not readily tip over. If the table lamp seems likely to slip off the polished top of the bedside table, an inconspicuous disk of high-friction flexible plastic sheet material can be placed under it.

What kind of lamp is best for bedhead lights?

It seems that most people prefer to use an ordinary filament lamp in their bedside light. It would be difficult to make an economic case for using compact fluorescent lamps (see Chapter 11) in bedside lamps, for the hours of use per annum are few, and the savings would be small. Filament lamps have the advantage that they can be used with simple and economical dimmers.

Some modern bedroom furniture ranges provide two separately switched miniature shaded directable spotlights, each containing a blown-glass reflector spotlamp or a low-voltage tungsten-halogen spotlamp to enable either person in a double bed to read without disturbing the other. If these are provided with deep reflectors to shield the lamps from view, they can be very effective.

How might dimming be used in lighting a bedroom?

For bedside lighting, a filament lamp has the advantage that – if one wishes – it can be operated in conjunction with an economically priced dimmer which allows the lamp to be adjusted from full brightness down to the merest glimmer. Dimmed down, the lamp can remain on all night without disturbing the sleeper – a great comfort in a time of sickness, or for an elderly person who may have to get up in the night. The dimmer may be located in the base of the bedside lamp, or may be of a type that fits into the lampholder below the lamp, or it may be fitted in the flexible lead to the fitting.

It is also possible to dim permanently installed room lighting (ceiling-mounted or wall-mounted lights) by installing a dimmer unit in place of the usual wall switch (see Chapter 13) – a feature of value in the bedrooms of small children.

How can one provide good lighting at the dressing table mirror?

The Victorian-style lady's dressing table has a central tilting mirror and two hinged side mirrors, and is customarily located in front of the bedroom window, with a shaded pendant light over it. Such an arrangement gives superb visibility during the day, but when there is no daylight it gives the lady no help at all with her make-up, for the light from above her head throws her eye sockets and neck into shadow, and emphasises her wrinkles!

Theatre people have long known that the best lighting for making up the face (and for shaving) is to have the light flowing horizontally to your face – even if it is rather glaring. Theatre dressing-room mirrors are fixed flat on the wall, and surrounded by bare filament lamps. Such units are available, but some people prefer to employ two small fittings containing tubular fluorescent lamps with wraparound diffusers, mounted vertically on either

RIGHT: As people in the theatre have long known, the best lighting for making-up the face is for the light to flow horizontally towards you - even if it is rather glaring.

BELOW: Mirror lights used in the bathroom must be of a pattern that is certified by the maker as being safe for use in steamy bathroom conditions.

side of the mirror, perhaps with a third unit of the same kind placed horizontally above – or below – the mirror.

Excellent results can be achieved by mounting two enclosed diffusing-globe fittings on the wall, on either side of the mirror and a little higher than eye level. The lamps used may be 60 W filament lamps or compact fluorescent lamps of the equivalent light output (see Figure 11.5).

Caution: Bedroom mirror lighting may employ types of lighting fittings that are suitable for use in ordinary dry interiors, but which may not be safe for use in bathrooms.

What are the lighting needs for the bedroom of an adolescent or school-age child?

An important requirement is to provide safe and adequate lighting at the desk used for homework and hobbies.

A convenient way of providing lighting at a desk is to position one or more fluorescent tubular lamps on the underside of a shelf above the desk.

The lamps should be shielded from view by a wooden canopy, in a manner similar to that used for lighting worktops in kitchens by concealing lamps under kitchen wall cabinets (see Chapter 4).

Many young people have a home computer which is used for study or for computer games. Because there may be annoying reflections from the screen, children tend to switch off the room lighting, but it is not good for vision to watch a computer screen or TV screen in a darkened room, the contrast between the screen brightness and the general room brightness being so great. It is always better to provide some subdued light. For this purpose, in most cases it will not be necessary to install a dimmer; it will be quite sufficient to use a carefully positioned portable table lamp or a directable desk lamp with its beam directed upward and away from the computer screen.

When working at a computer, it is essential to be provided with a reasonable level of lighting on papers or books to which the user needs to refer while working at the screen, and an adjustable desk lamp can provide this.

The methods of providing lighting for reading in bed are discussed earlier in this chapter.

Although such lighting would not be suitable for long hours of use, a shaded table-lamp casting its intimate light on a desk gives a feeling of privacy.

How should small children's bedrooms be lit?

Children are particularly vulnerable to electric shock, and all electrical appliances have some degree of inherent danger. Children will investigate them, using their fingers and mouths, and probing with any handy object. Therefore, any electric nightlight that the child could possibly touch must be constructed so well that it could fall repeatedly from the table without damage, and it must be impossible for a small child to open it to get access

Good lighting in a child's room will encourage reading, and protect against eye-strain.

to the hot lamp or to the electrical connections. Preferably, any bedside lamp for a small child's room should use a low-wattage 12 V filament lamp, and be supplied through a plug-top step-down transformer to reduce the supply voltage to 12 volts so that the lamp would be safe to the child – even if taken into a wet bed.

The preferred method of providing a comforting glow of light in a small child's bedroom is by fitting a 5 W neon glow lamp in a ceiling-mounted lighting fitting. This will suffuse the room in a pink glow which is sufficient for a child's reassurance, and very cosy in appearance when contained in a suitable shade which allows light to flow up to the ceiling, and which shields the lamp from the child's view from its bed. Also available are small self-contained nightlight units containing a glow lamp which plug into a 13 A socket.

BATHROOMS

What safety precautions are necessary in choosing lighting equipment for the bathroom?

To prevent risk of electric shock due to the presence of moisture, all lighting fittings used in bathrooms should be of enclosed construction and specifically stated by the supplier to have a degree of 'ingress protection' suitable for use in bathrooms (i.e. steam-proof and splash-proof). Do not position any lighting fitting within touching distance of a person taking a shower, nor where the fitting may be splashed in use unless it is specifically certified by the maker as being suitable for use within a shower cubicle.

If the lighting switch must be located within the bathroom it should be a ceiling-mounted pull-cord switch. It is understood that it is permissible to mount a light switch within a bathroom provided that it is out of the reach of a person in the bath or shower, but the authors do not recommend this; preferably any wall switch will be mounted outside the bathroom, where a standard-pattern wall switch may be used. The same provisions apply to switches that control fixed high-level heating devices such as infra-red lamps (which provide both light and heat) and quartz-lamp infra-red radiant heaters. Portable heating devices and mains-voltage radios, etc., should never be taken into a bathroom. No socket outlets (other than a shaver socket) should be installed in a bathroom.

What are the lighting requirements in the bathroom?

The lighting level needed in a domestic bathroom of typical size and of light-coloured decor can be achieved by using one or more lamps giving a total output of around 1,000 lumens. This requirement will be met by having one ceiling-mounted enclosed diffusing fitting containing a 100 W filament lamp, or two units each containing a 60 W filament lamp. The same results can be achieved using much less energy by having one lighting fitting containing a compact fluorescent lamp, or possibly by two units each containing a lamp of this type (see Figure 11.5); however, the bathroom is not a very cost-effective place to install CFLs as the periods of use are so short.

A light at the mirror over the wash-hand basin is very useful, and for this purpose a *shaver light* or *bathroom mirror light* may be used. This must be certified by the maker as designed to be safe to use in bathrooms. Preferably select a pattern that has a built-in switch which isolates the unit when the cover is opened, thus making it safe to open the unit to replace the lamp. Typical fittings house a small fluorescent lamp or architectural tubular lamp ('striplight'), and may incorporate a single-voltage or dual-voltage socket outlet for use with an electric shaver.

Caution: Do not attempt to plug anything into a bathroom shaver socket other than an electric razor designed for the supply voltage. Do not have any other socket outlets in the bathroom, and never introduce any kind of mains-operated portable light or electrical appliance into the bathroom.

Bathroom mirror lights incorporating an electric shaver socket are available with an internal switch to electrically isolate the unit when it is opened for relamping.

What precautions should be taken when replacing failed lamps in the bathroom?

When replacing a lamp in a bathroom lighting fitting, prevent any risk of electric shock by switching off the mains, or switching off the relevant circuit at the consumer unit. This precaution is necessary on two grounds: first, the damp conditions generally found in bathrooms increase the risk of electric shock if there should be a defect in the wiring or if the lamp should be broken; second, if the lighting fitting is switched by a pull-cord ceiling-mounted switch, when the lamp has failed it is impossible to know whether the circuit is live or not.

Lighting for
ENTRANCES, STAIRS
and PASSAGES

Placing a lighting fitting under a staircase brings into use what would otherwise be a 'dead' space, for example to accommodate hats and coats, shelving or other storage units.

What are the important considerations in lighting for an entrance hall?

The entrance hall is the ideal location for using compact fluorescent lamps, since the lights are burning for long hours. The lighting for an entrance hall should be planned in conjunction with that of the porch or external steps (see Chapter 8). It is important for security to be able to see who is calling at the door at night, so the porch lighting should be arranged so that light is cast on visitors to enable them to be seen from inside the house, through a front window, through an optical spy-hole, or through a clear or translucent panel in the front door. Many homes these days are fitted with a miniature video security scanner, the camera for which can only function if there is adequate external lighting.

It is desirable that the lighting first seen by visitors as they enter the home is warm and welcoming, and gives a first impression of comfort and welcome. If there is a mirror in the hall, it could be a good idea to place a light over it so that arriving and departing guests – and occupants – can see themselves comfortably.

The lighting in the entrance hall may contribute to the illumination of the stairs. It is therefore wise to arrange that, when the hall lights are turned off, there is always adequate illumination on the stairs for safety.

How might one light a long passage?

A straight, level, uncluttered corridor or passageway within a dwelling does not require a high standard of lighting to ensure safety. If the lights are left on throughout the hours of darkness (or continuously if little daylight enters), the installation of a few downlighters fitted with low-power compact fluorescent lamps would be appropriate and economical to operate.

Passageways cannot be furnished to make them seem more comfortable, for occasional tables, plants, etc., would be obstructions. However, it is possible to cheer up a bare passageway by hanging a few pictures and providing them with picture lights, which are attractive to look at and contribute some light to the floor.

What are the requirements for lighting stairs?

Steps and stairs are seen more clearly if the lighting is arranged as far as possible to leave the risers of the steps in comparative darkness, so that the noses of the treads are more clearly seen (see Figure 6.1).

In multistorey buildings, the lights on landings should be arranged so as not to be too glaring to persons as they pass up or down the stairs. Shaded pendant lighting fittings may be appropriate. Light colours for the ceiling and walls, and clean surfaces, will reflect more light and make the stairway safer. If there is a dark stair carpet, painting the exposed portions of the steps on each side of the carpet a light colour will aid visibility.

Additional illumination can be provided in an attractive manner by the spill light from picture lights as described, or by installing suitable wall lights. If there is a window alongside a tall staircase, an attractive treatment could be to install a pelmet light (as described in Chapter 14) to make an interesting feature and also to throw some additional light onto the stairway.

If staircases and passageways are lit with the use of compact fluorescent lamps, their low running cost will enable the lights to be kept on continuously from dusk to bedtime – or even from dusk to breakfast time – without great expense.

A corridor or staircase that would be the exit route from the premises in an emergency might be fitted with *emergency lighting*. See the note on this in Chapter 2, and the guidance on installing emergency lighting given in Chapter 14.

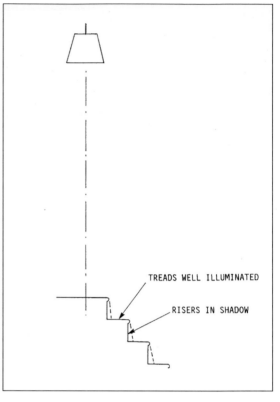

TREADS WELL ILLUMINATED

RISERS IN SHADOW

FIGURE 6.1
A lighting fitting over a flight of stairs should preferably be positioned slightly back from the edge of the top step so as to light the treads, but to leave the risers in comparative shadow.

CHAPTER 7

Lighting for the GARAGE *or* WORKSHOP

What lighting is needed over the garage doors?

It is useful to install a lighting fitting over the garage doors, or, if an up-and-over door is fitted, at one side of the door at door-head height. This will provide sufficient light for loading the car, and for checking the oil, water, etc., when the car is parked outside the garage.

The fitting for this purpose should be an 'exterior-use' pattern of bulk-head fitting, enclosed in a glass or plastic diffuser, or an enclosed exterior-pattern 'jam-jar' fitting mounted on a wall bracket, or attached by its integral means of mounting to a vertical surface if so provided.

If the fitting will only be used occasionally, it may be fitted with a 60 W filament lamp. If it will be left on for long hours or all night, select a fitting suitable for a compact fluorescent lamp of around 800 lumens (see table of compact fluorescent lamps in Figure 11.5). Remember that in cold weather a filament lamp will come to full brightness immediately on being switched on, while a compact fluorescent lamp will take some minutes to come to full brightness.

If one has a remotely controlled 'up-and-over' garage door, it is very convenient if the light over the door is switched on automatically by the operation of the remote-control device that controls the doors. In one system, the light remains on while the door is open, and automatically extinguishes three minutes after the door is closed. If no such system is in use, the light over the garage door may be switched from a position near the rear door of the house, or two-position switching may be employed, with one switch placed near the rear of the house and one outside the garage door. The switches would require to be of a pattern suitable for exterior use. (Two-position switching is described in Chapter 14.)

Are there any special electrical risks in a garage or workshop?

Yes. Because the garage is an 'earthy' environment, the risk of electric shock is high if proper precautions are not taken. If your home electrical installation does not include an RCD in or near the consumer unit, it is recommended that one be installed at the point where power is brought into the garage, or that a plug-in RCD device be used in any socket in the garage to which any load is connected.

How could one provide good lighting at a workbench?

A workbench in the garage can be lit satisfactorily for most household repair jobs and hobbies if it is illuminated with a single-lamp fitting for a 1,200 mm 36 W fluorescent tubular lamp. An economical pattern would be a fitting designed for industrial use and provided with a slotted metal trough reflector. Because the garage is not heated, there may be condensation in the winter, so it is desirable to employ only lighting fittings that are suitable for use in damp conditions.

The fitting should be mounted above the bench and parallel to it, with its centre 150 mm to 300 mm in from the front edge of the bench. A suitable mounting height would be 2 m from the floor to the underside of the fitting. In that position, it will give sufficient light for routine maintenance work when the car is placed so that the engine is adjacent to the bench.

A safe way of switching the bench light would be by a pull-cord switch mounted on the ceiling or a roof beam.

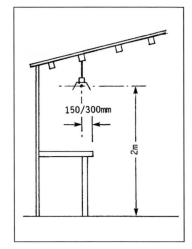

FIGURE 7.1 LIGHTING A BENCH
Lighting at a bench in the garage or workshop by use of a 1200mm 36W fluorescent tubular lamp in an industrial type reflector fitting.

How might one have an electrically safe portable hand lamp for use in the garage?

The safest kind of hand lamp for garage use is one made for a 12 V supply, which is clipped onto the car battery or connected to the 12 V output terminals of a battery charger.

If a mains-voltage hand lamp is used, it should be connected by a robust heavy-duty plastic-coated flexible lead (not house-wiring cable or ordinary lighting flex), fitted with a three-pin plug and 3 A fuse. Hand lamps of 'double-insulated' construction, in which the lamp is protected by a tough plastic enclosure, may be provided with a two-core flexible cable and do not need an earth connection; in such a case, the two cores should be connected to the 'L' and 'N' terminals in the three-pin plug. (Wiring-up of three-pin plugs is explained in Chapter 14.)

Hand lamps that have a wire cage around the lamp, and hand lamps (other than double-insulated patterns) that do not have proper provision for earthing, are potential killers. Hand lamps occasionally get dropped; a hand lamp containing a broken lamp should not be touched until it has been isolated from the mains by withdrawing the plug from the socket outlet.

An excellent type of hand lamp for domestic use contains a small fluorescent tubular lamp and its control gear encapsulated in a tough, clear plastic sheath. When the lamp eventually reaches the end of its long life, the whole hand lamp is discarded. These hand lamps are waterproof and very robust, and in domestic conditions of use will give many years of service before they need to be replaced.

How might one conveniently provide some extra socket outlets at the workshop bench?

You might wish to be able to plug in an adjustable lamp for use at the bench, as well as to provide supplies for things such as a glue-pot, a soldering iron or an electric drill. The important thing is not to improvise wiring if you need to supply additional outlets, but to do the job safely. In Chapter 14 we discuss the use of *trailing sockets*. Additional sockets can easily be provided in the garage by use of a four-gang trailing socket device which could be attached to the wall behind the bench and fed from an existing socket. Some patterns of trailing socket device are provided with two keyhole slots on the back for ease of mounting. These slots fit over the two screws that you will put in the wall, so the device is securely held, but can be readily removed if required.

EXTERIOR *lighting*

Why might one wish to install some outdoor lighting?

Outdoor lighting may be installed for entirely practical reasons, or it may be provided mainly for pleasure; many installations combine both utility and attractiveness.

At the front of the house, outdoor lighting may be employed to identify the house and to make the approach to it safe and welcoming for visitors. If you live in a village or a street that has little or no public lighting, you may wish to provide some welcoming lights at the front of your house from dusk to bedtime every evening.

Outdoor lighting at the rear of the house will make it safer to go out to the dustbin or the back gate at night. Suitable lighting can impart a delightful appearance to the night-time garden at all seasons and in all weathers. Viewed from the warm comfort inside the house, a floodlit garden under a sprinkling of snow looks like Fairyland!

Does the standard of nearby streetlighting affect the security of homes?

Yes, and sometimes very much so. If you live in an urban area, the lighting of the roads and footpaths near your home will certainly affect the level of security at night. Unless you live on a main trunk road, the streetlighting near your house is the responsibility of your local authority.

If there is no streetlighting near your home, or if the local streetlighting is of a poor standard, and if the people in your community wish to have some installed or have existing streetlighting improved, the householders whose premises are affected could make a joint approach to their local authority to request that improvements be made. However, note that the local authority may decide that the requested work cannot be carried out without a contribution towards the cost from the 'frontagers' who will benefit from the improvements.

On grounds of economy, side-street lighting in many local authority areas is switched off at midnight or perhaps at 1 a.m. Over many years there has been strong pressure on local authorities to cease this practice, for the

As darkness falls, the welcoming lights symbolise our instinctive feelings about the comforts of home. External lighting, if switched by a PE controller, will help protect against night prowlers - even when the family is away from home.

police have repeatedly stated that the frequency of burglary, and of breaking into or theft of cars, is significantly higher during the hours that the streets are in darkness. In some areas, the local authority will agree to change from part-night to all-night streetlighting if the frontagers agree to help with the cost – which, if efficient lamps are used in the streetlighting lanterns, can be quite a small annual charge per house.

If you live in an unlit street, or if the rear of your premises is in darkness at night, you should certainly consider installing some security lighting.

What is security lighting?

Security lighting is outdoor lighting, the prime function of which is to protect the premises from prowlers and burglars at night. Of course, we know that many incidents of housebreaking occur during daylight hours, but the crime prevention officer of your local police will doubtless confirm that the

57

risks of a night-time criminal attack against your home are likely to be significantly diminished if you install some outside lighting that is in operation every night of the year, from dusk to dawn. Such lighting is termed 'security lighting'.

Manually switched exterior lighting, and lighting that is switched on by a passive infra-red (PIR) proximity detector when someone approaches, has its value; but, by our definition, it is not security lighting. Be cautious about advertisements for lighting fittings with integral PIR switching which are claimed to be 'security lights'. There are some exterior floodlights on the market that have integral PIR switching which are also intended to act as a crude sort of intruder alarm by sounding a buzzer when the lamp is activated. No PIR device will invariably distinguish between human beings and passing cats (or a fox having a look round your garden in the night!) so false alarms are likely to be frequent, and such a fitting is likely to be a nuisance both to you and your neighbours.

In order to provide reliable all-night operation, security lighting systems may be switched automatically by a *photoelectric switch* (PE switch) which responds to the absence or presence of daylight, so it is not necessary to remember to switch them on and off. Indeed, the lights will still come on when you are away from home, which is an added security benefit. PE switching is more reliable than time switches, which, having to embody seasonal day-length adjustment, are quite expensive.

Surely, it would be very costly to have security lighting that is on all night, every night?

Not at all. As many householders have discovered, the cost of security lighting is a small price to pay for peace of mind. Despite the long hours of operation, if modern energy-efficient lamps are used, the energy consumed by two or three security lights around your home will not present a great expense. For example, if your installation comprised two lighting fittings, each containing a compact fluorescent lamp rated at 16 W, the energy consumed in a year of all-night operation would be only 140 kWh (units). And, if you purchase your electricity on a two-part tariff, the lamps would be operating on cheap night-rate electricity for a large proportion of the hours of use.

What types of lighting fittings might be used in domestic outdoor lighting?

There is an enormously wide choice of suitable exterior lighting equipment for these applications, ranging from utilitarian and economical patterns of bulkhead fittings and 'jam-jar' fittings, to quite luxurious antique reproduction lanterns in many forms.

ABOVE RIGHT: Path lights, recessed into the ground, guide one's footsteps safely. Their upward flow of light also charmingly illuminates the nearby greenery.

RIGHT: Little knee-high illuminated bollards, attractive in themselves, will safely light one's way along a path or drive at night.

OVERLEAF

LEFT: There are styles of external lighting fittings to suit all situations. Inconspicuous during the day, they help to make the garden into an 'outdoor room'.

RIGHT: Even in the English climate, lighting will extend the hours during which the garden can be enjoyed - if only as a spectacle to view from within the warmth of the house!

Outdoor lighting can be stylish and elegant, as well as useful. There is a wide choice of traditional designs of lighting fittings such as reproduction carriage lamps for wall mounting, as well as reproductions of traditional lamp posts, all of which can house very efficient modern lamps. There are also extensive ranges of modern lighting fittings for outdoor use, so it is always possible to find fittings that will do the lighting job you have in mind as well as harmonising with the architectural style of your home. Outside lighting, even if provided primarily for security, can be highly decorative. Layouts and methods of installing domestic exterior lighting installations are reviewed in Chapter 15.

How might security lighting be arranged for a larger area – say, a common entrance area to a block of flats, or a communal car park?

Where there is a space to which a number of homes have access as at some blocks of flats, or if it is desired to protect a parking area shared by a number of dwellings, the security lighting arrangements have to be somewhat different to those for a single dwelling. Advice should be sought from the crime prevention officer of the police in your district. If the area is the responsibility of your local authority, perhaps you can persuade them to light it. If the cost of the lighting must be shared by the users, proposals and quotations for schemes of lighting may be prepared by lighting companies, by electrical contractors, or by your electricity supply company.

How might one arrange some floodlighting for the garden?

For typical suburban gardens, one or two small floodlight fittings mounted on the back wall of the house will provide sufficient light for enjoyment of the garden at night, for moving about safely, and to enable a patio area to be used for barbecues, etc. The method of doing this is given in Chapter 15.

How might one light a long front drive or path?

It is not necessary to use a great deal of light in order to create safe conditions for walking along a drive or path. In many applications it is possible to site one or two miniature 'illuminated bollards' or 'path lights' along the path or drive at strategic positions.

What sort of lamps might be used in outdoor lighting fittings?

For lights that are to be operated for long hours, the best choice will be one of the patterns of compact fluorescent lamps which are reviewed in Chapter 11. They are economical to operate and require very infrequent replacement.

For manually switched lights, or for lamps to be controlled by a PIR

proximity detector, it would be better to use filament lamps. The reason for this is that filament lamps come to full brightness immediately upon being switched on, whereas compact fluorescent lamps can take a minute to come to full brightness (and rather longer in very cold weather). Further, as the total number of hours of use per annum will be quite small, the additional cost of a compact fluorescent lamp could not be justified.

60

There is something particularly dramatic about the sight of a tree - at any season of the year - illuminated with one or two green floodlamps directed up into it.

For garden floodlighting and patio lighting, tungsten-halogen lamps are ideally suitable to use in small floodlights as described in Chapter 15. PAR floodlamps may be used with excellent decorative effect in gardens, perhaps in 'garden spikes'.

How could one have some temporary decorative lighting in the garden?

Two types of decorative lighting that can be employed in the garden are spike lamps and festoon lighting.

A *spike lamp* is just what it sounds like, a lamp on a spike. These simple and economical fittings are a very attractive way of introducing decorative lighting into the garden.

The body of the spike lamp is a robust plastic enclosure which houses an ES (screw-type) lampholder for an 80 W PAR reflector lamp. A swivel permits the beam of the lamp to be directed up or down as desired, and the whole fitting can be turned on its spike when it is planted in the ground.

Eighty-watt PAR lamps are available in a range of colours, so a really festive appearance can be contrived. There is something particularly charming about the sight of a tree – at any season of the year – illuminated with one or two green PAR lamps directed up into its branches.

Spike lamps provide an attractive method for putting temporary lighting onto a garden pond (especially in the late spring when the frogs are active!). Plant the spike in the ground near the edge of the pond, and set the beam to skim across the water. Some very pretty effects can be created by directing coloured PAR lamp beams into the spray of a garden fountain. Lighting the pond is an entertaining feature if you have people coming to see the garden after dark. The method of installing spike lamps is described in Chapter 15.

Festoon lighting consists of a length of cable having a series of small lighting fittings or special waterproof lampholders permanently attached to it at short intervals along its length. A mixture of differently coloured lamps may be used, or the covers of the small lighting fittings may be randomly coloured. Festoons are usually used more for their pretty appearance than for the light they shed. Note that the same festoon could double for brightening and adorning the garden on summer nights and for decorating an outdoor Christmas tree.

There are a number of different types of festoon lighting on the market, including systems that give a fairground appearance and seem to be generally more suitable for a garden party than for gently lighting the garden. For example, some festoons provide flashing lights and sequence switching systems which give the appearance of light running along the festoon. Other festoon systems can be fitted with coloured or white lamps, and can be used without a flasher, to provide some very pretty lighting effects.

Some safety notes on the use of festoon lighting are given in Chapter 15.

Is it a practical proposition to install lighting in a garden shed or in the greenhouse?

Yes, but installing electric cabling between the house and the shed or greenhouse is a job for a properly qualified electrician. A supply to the shed and greenhouse will enable the use of Gro-Lux (tm) lamps (see Chapter 11) and for tasks to be done when daylight has faded. Having one or two socket outlets in the shed will facilitate using electric tools, while in the greenhouse they can supply heated seed germinators. See Chapter 15 for some guidelines.

Can lighting be provided for an outdoor swimming pool?

Yes, but the installation of such lighting is a job for a properly qualified electrician. The special requirements are outlined in Chapter 15.

However, new developments are on the way, in the form of fibre-optic lighting which can enable light to be 'piped' considerable distances (see Chapter 2). By this means, the lamp may be installed safely in the house, and the light conducted by the optical fibres to the outdoor location where it is to be used. Because no electrical conductors would be taken into the garden, the system would be free of all risk of electric shock – even if the fibre-optic light guides were actually immersed in the pool!

Festoon lights, trailed through the shrubs, are unnoticeable by day. After dusk they create a colourful sight that will tempt you to have an evening garden party.

PART 2

PRACTICAL MATTERS AND USEFUL INFORMATION FOR DIY

This part expands the basic ideas given in Part 1, and gives guidelines for DIY. It includes explanations of practical matters which will be well within the scope of most DIY enthusiasts.

Some BASIC IDEAS *about* ELECTRICITY *in the* HOME

Is the electricity supply company that provides power to my home responsible for the safety of my electrical installation?

No. The Electricity Supply Regulations 1988 govern the supply of electricity by the electricity supply company to your premises, but the responsibility of the electricity supply company stops at the meter. However, the electricity supply company has the right to disconnect you from their supply if they consider your installation to be unsafe.

Who is responsible for the safety of the electrical wiring in my home?

You, the occupier, are responsible. Because a faulty electrical installation could be the cause of fire or electric shock, you will be wise to employ a properly qualified electrician to undertake any required changes to the permanent wiring.

How can I ensure that my lighting installation is safe?

The safety of the lighting system in your home should be your prime consideration. Many useful additions to home lighting installations can be achieved without changing the permanent wiring, and can be done safely if you follow the instructions given in the text. Some general safety advice is given in Chapter 16. However, people without electrical training should not undertake alterations or additions to the fixed electrical installations in their homes, but should employ a properly qualified electrician to do such work.

Anything less than the highest possible standard of electrical safety could create a fire risk, or expose people to danger of electric shock, children and elderly people being particularly at risk. Most electrical accidents and fires due to defective wiring or faulty lighting fittings are preventable by good practice, e.g. by using the correct size of fuse and the use of protective devices which are explained in this chapter.

How can I be sure that the contractor I employ is a properly qualified electrician?

Companies that are members of the Electrical Contractors Association (ECA), or the ECA of Scotland, employ trained people to carry out their work. You can inspect the list of members of the ECA in most public libraries. Many reputable electrical contractors are certified by the National Inspection Council for Electrical Installation Contracting (NICEIC). Competent electrical contractors will certify that their work complies with British Standard 7671 which embodies the *Wiring Regulations* issued by the Institution of Electrical Engineers (IEE).

What happens to the electrical energy consumed by lamps?

The function of a lamp is to convert electrical energy into light energy. Lamps do this with greater or less efficacy according to their type (see Chapter 11). All the energy that goes into any electrical appliance can be accounted for. In lamps, only a small proportion is emitted as visible light, the remainder being emitted as heat. The energy emitted as light is also eventually converted to heat, for when light is reflected, a proportion of it is converted to heat at each reflection, and eventually all the light is so converted.

As a byproduct of the production of light, the energy consumed by the lamps you use contributes to the heating of your home. The heat output from ten 100 W lamps is exactly the same as that from a 1 kW heater element.

Lighting fittings are designed to allow the heat from the lamp to be safely dissipated by radiation and convection. For this reason, lamps should not be operated in small unventilated spaces, and fittings should never be covered, for this could cause overheating.

What are watts?

Power is the rate at which electrical energy is consumed by a lamp or by any other electrical appliance. Power consumption is measured in *watts* (symbol W). For example, a 100 W lamp consumes energy at a rate of four times faster than a 25 W lamp. Most people are familiar with the idea of a one-kilowatt electric heater element; a kilowatt (symbol kW) is one thousand watts.

How are we charged for the electrical energy we use?

Operating a 1 kW appliance for one hour will consume one kilowatt-hour (symbol kWh), also called 'a unit'. For one unit, you could operate a 1 kW fire for one hour, or a 100 W lamp for ten hours, or a 25 W lamp for forty hours.

The electricity meter in your home records how many units (kWh) have been consumed and have to be paid for. Your electricity supply company will provide you with details of the tariff that applies to your premises. Since April 1994, value-added tax (VAT) has been charged on fuel bills. As well as a charge per unit consumed, the tariff may include a standing quarterly charge (which is payable however much or little electricity you use). The unit charge may vary according to the time of day; for example, if you are on a two-part tariff, the cost per unit will be lower at night between stated times, or the times may vary but the length of the low-rate period remains constant.

What are amperes?

The size of an electrical current flowing in a circuit is measured in *amperes* (symbol A), often abbreviated to 'amps'.

The common three-pin socket outlets used in our homes are specified in British Standard 1363. They are rated at 13 A, i.e. the total amount of current that may be taken from a socket outlet must not exceed 13 amperes.

What are volts?

The electrical pressure that drives the electrical current around the circuits is measured in *volts* (symbol V). The single-phase supply to homes in the UK is operated at nominally either 230 V or 240 V. It is planned to standardise all domestic electrical supplies at 230 V. Your local electricity supply company will be able to tell you the voltage of your supply, and when a change – if any – will be carried out.

How does the voltage affect lighting?

When purchasing lamps or lighting fittings, check the labels to be sure that they are suitable for the supply voltage at your address.

Generally, operating any kind of lamp rated at 240 V on a 230 V supply is not harmful; it will tend to extend the lamp life (especially so in the case of filament lamps), but inevitably there is a reduction in light output. Compact fluorescent lamps and tubular fluorescent lamps may be difficult to start if operated below their rated voltage, especially when they are cold.

If you operate any type of lamp rated at 230 V on a 240 V supply, its life will tend to be shortened, particularly in the case of filament lamps. For efficient operation, compact fluorescent lamps and tubular fluorescent lamps should only be used at their rated voltages.

How are watts, amperes and volts related?

One watt of energy is consumed when an electrical current of one ampere flows due to an electrical pressure of one volt. In any circuit, *watts = volts* x *amperes*. Thus, if we know any two of these three values, we can easily calculate the other one.

What do fuses do?

A fuse is a device to protect against the effects of excessive current. It is a deliberate 'weak link' which stops the current flowing in a circuit if too big a load is connected to it, or because there is an electrical fault causing excessive current to flow.

When electrical current flows along a conductor (e.g. any wire, or the element in a heater), heat is generated. The temperature rise of the wiring in your house under normal conditions is negligible; but fuses are designed to heat up rapidly when a current greater than the rated current passes through them. The conductor in the fuse 'blows' (melts) and isolates the circuit from the supply.

The electricity supply company's main fuse is located near your meter. It is connected to the distribution board (consumer unit) which contains fuses or MCBs (miniature circuit-breakers – another kind of protective device described in this chapter) to protect your installation.

The ring-main which supplies the socket outlets in your home is protected by a fuse or an MCB in the consumer unit. The fuse for each appliance that is connected to a socket outlet is located in the plug-top.

How can one choose the correct size of fuse to go into a plug-top?

The standard sizes of cartridge fuses to go into BS 1363 three-pin plug-tops are 3 amperes, 5 amperes, 10 amperes and 13 amperes. When you buy a lighting fitting which is supplied complete with a three-pin plug, or if you buy such a plug separately, the chances are that you will find that the supplier has fitted it with a 13 A fuse. This is not good practice, for single lighting fittings of types used in the home, and even domestic lighting circuits supplying several lamps, rarely need a fuse bigger than the 3 A size.

The matter seems to baffle many home handypersons because lamps are sized by the *power* they consume (watts), while fuses are sized by the *current* they can carry (amperes). To understand it, all we need to appreciate is that if we know the power rating in watts of a lighting fitting or an appliance, we can easily calculate its current consumption, and then be able to select the correct size of fuse. For example, if we wanted to know the current consumption of a 100 W lamp on a voltage of 230 V, we could calculate: 100 W divided by 230 V = 0.43 A, so we would select the next highest rating of fuse (in this case the smallest in the range) the 3 A size.

For standard 230 V/240 V supplies, we do not need to do such a calculation, but can use the following table:

For a total load of:	Use fuse size:
Up to 690 watts	3 amperes
690 to 1150 watts	5 amperes
1150 to 2300 watts	10 amperes
2300 to 3000 watts	13 amperes

In practice it is unlikely that any lighting circuit in your home will have a total load of more than 690 watts, so the 3 A fuse will be the size you should routinely place in all three-pin plug-tops that supply power to lighting.

What is a miniature circuit-breaker (MCB)?

If you have any rewirable fuses in your home electrical installation, you are advised to employ a properly qualified electrician to replace the fuseboard with a modern *consumer unit* (domestic electrical distribution panel) fitted with *miniature circuit-breakers* (MCBs).

An MCB is a type of switch which is also a protective device, for it serves the same purpose as a fuse. It is in fact a switch that can be turned on and off by moving a lever. If the switch is in the ON position and an excessive current flows, the device detects this and 'trips', i.e. it switches itself off rapidly to prevent damage to the wiring and to any connected appliances.

Modern 'consumer units' (electrical distribution units) are so neat that they may be located in a conveniently accessible position and not hidden in a cupboard.

MCBs are simple to operate, and are easily reset after tripping. Unlike a fuse, when they 'trip' (cut the power), there is nothing to replace.

Modern mains distribution boards are called 'consumer units', and have an MCB to protect each circuit. The consumer unit is usually located near your electricity meter, but modern ones are so neat that they may be located in a conveniently accessible position and not hidden in a cupboard. A consumer unit usually has a master switch to turn off the power to all the circuits it controls. Modern ones also incorporate a *residual current device* (RCD).

What is a residual current device (RCD)?

Under normal conditions, the current flowing into a circuit from the 'live' side of the mains flows to the 'neutral' line, so that the currents in the 'live' and 'neutral' leads are equal. If there is an 'earth fault', current flows from some part of the circuit to 'earth', a dangerous condition which could cause fire or electric shock. The function of a residual current device (RCD) is to detect any such flow of electricity from the system to earth, and to isolate the system from the mains automatically and very rapidly.

RCDs are potential life-savers, and their use is recommended by the Royal Society for the Prevention of Accidents. It would be wise to have one fitted to protect at least the socket-outlet circuits in your home. One RCD across all the circuits is definitely not recommended, particularly if you have electric cooking and water heating. All new home wiring installations must comply with the current edition of the *Wiring Regulations*, and are required to have RCD protection.

If you have an an electric mower or other electrical appliance which is used outdoors and connected to a socket outlet, you would be wise to have an RCD fitted or use an *RCD adaptor* at the socket. RCD adaptors are plug-in devices which work on the same principle as permanently installed RCDs. They provide added circuit protection against electrocution. Their use is recommended for use with all appliances around the home (including portable lighting fittings and Christmas tree lights), and – especially – for protection of circuits to electric mowers and hedge trimmers where there is the danger of electrocution through the cable being cut.

Before using an RCD adaptor, read and follow carefully the instructions issued by the manufacturer with regard to its testing and use. To use an RCD adaptor, follow this procedure:

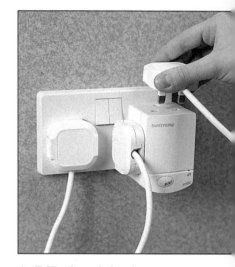

An 'RCD adaptor' plugs into any socket outlet, to provide protection against an earth-leakage fault which would create danger of electric shock.

1. If the lighting fitting is not already provided with a flexible cable and a fused three-pin plug, connect a flexible cable correctly to the lighting fitting and replace any cover that has been removed.

2. Fit a three-pin plug to the other end of the flexible cable, ensuring that it contains the correct size of fuse.

3. Ensure that the switch on the 13 A socket outlet is OFF.

4. Insert the RCD adaptor into the socket outlet.

5. Insert the plug of the extension lead into the RCD adaptor.

6. Switch on.

Lighting engineers use an instrument called a 'lightmeter' to measure illuminance. This is placed at the point where the measurement is wanted, and the reading in lux is read from the scale. Note: A lightmeter is not the same as a photographic exposure meter which measures brightness, not illuminance.

How is brightness measured?

Measurement of brightness is outside the scope of this book, but it can be helpful to understand that the brightness we see on a surface always results from a combination of two factors – the reflection factor of the surface (dark surfaces reflecting less light), and the light flowing onto it, i.e. the illuminance (lux). For example, the same brightness would result from a white non-shiny surface with a reflection factor of 100 per cent being illuminated to 1 lux, as from a non-shiny surface with a reflection factor of 50 per cent being illuminated to 2 lux, etc.

What are the attributes of brightness?

Brightness has two attributes, *luminance* and *luminosity*. Luminance is the measurable factor referred to in the previous answer. Luminosity is a subjective attribute, and our assessment of it varies with our state of adaptation at that instant. For example, a candle flame seems barely luminous when seen in bright sunshine, but it would seem very bright if it were brought into a totally dark room where we had been for some time and our eyes had become adapted to the dark conditions. In both cases the luminance of the candle flame would be the same, but its luminosity (i.e. how bright it seemed to our eyes) would be much greater in the second case.

What is glare?

As explained in Chapter 2, we experience glare when some part of our visual field is excessively bright compared with the illuminance to which our eyes are adapted at the time. We suffer 'direct glare' when a bright lamp or lighting fitting is seen against too dark a background. The main way in which we control direct glare is by choosing lighting fittings that shield the lamp from direct view.

We may suffer 'indirect glare' from the reflection of a bright source on a glossy surface such as a polished tabletop or shiny paper (see Figure 10.2). Indirect glare can be minimised by using enclosed diffusing light-

FIGURE 10.2
Direct and indirect glare. Direct glare can be reduced by limiting the brightness of the lightsource, or by lightening the colour of the background, or by directing more light to the background, i.e. reducing the brightness contrast between the lightsource and its background.

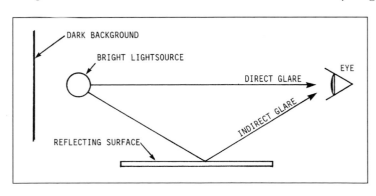

77

ing fittings, and by carefully siting them in relation to the task. In order to reduce the brightness of reflections of the lamps from shiny surfaces when filament lamps are used, it is generally better to choose lamps with 'pearl' or 'opal' envelopes, even though the diffusing envelope absorbs a small proportion of their light output. The problem of indirect glare is much diminished by changing to compact fluorescent lamps, for these have a lower intrinsic brightness (see Chapter 11).

How can a room be well lit without causing discomfort glare?

The first requirement is usually to place a shade, a reflector or diffuser around each lamp so that the lamp itself cannot be seen from normal angles of view. In most home situations, all kinds of lamps (including compact fluorescent lamps) are much too bright to be looked at directly. However, in small rooms – say, small kitchens – bare fluorescent lamps mounted on a white ceiling might be just tolerable if the lamps are well away from normal directions of view (see Chapter 4), but the use of diffusing enclosed fittings in such situations is strongly recommended.

As we explained in Chapter 2, glare is not caused by the amount of light, but by excessive contrasts in brightness. Thus, a bright lighting fitting could seem uncomfortably glaring if seen against dark furnishings, but more tolerable if seen against a light-coloured wall or ceiling.

Changing the lamps in your fittings to others of lower wattage will not reduce glare very much, but it will certainly reduce the illuminance and perhaps make the room look gloomy. With care in choosing the lighting fittings and in positioning them, as well as by choosing suitable room colours, it is possible to provide all the light needed for activities and tasks and for the good appearance of the interior without causing any noticeable glare. But don't overdo the reduction of glare to the point where you produce a bland, flat-looking interior.

If I light my room to a higher illuminance, will it look brighter?

Yes. Also, simply choosing lighter colours for the ceiling and walls (and for the carpet or flooring) will make the room look brighter, even if the amount of light has not been increased.

What illuminances do we commonly experience, indoors and outdoors?

Our eyes can adapt to a wide range of lighting conditions, from bright sunshine to faint starlight. Because our eyes adapt, we may not realise how great are the differences in illuminance between various situations. When we bask in English June sunshine, we are experiencing an illuminance of about 80,000 lux. On an overcast day out of doors, the illuminance may be about

5,000 lux, while 'bad light stops play' at around 1,000 lux. Compared with these figures, the lighting levels we use for general lighting in a domestic room are very small, say around 100 to 200 lux for general lighting, with perhaps up to about 500 lux in the light from a local fitting such as a reading lamp. Outdoors at night we will find that typical side-street lighting measures about 5 lux. Clear moonlight is about one-fifth of a lux, while clear starlight amounts to no more than a hundredth of a lux.

What determines how much light is needed for any place or task?

Because our eyes have the ability to adapt to low illuminances, once the process of dark adaption has taken place (which takes a minute or two), we are quite able to move about safely in an illuminance of a few lux. For example, we can safely move about in a bedroom lit only by the dim light from a 5 W neon glow lamp used as a nightlight – an illuminance about the same as moonlight.

When we are in a low illuminance, even though we have become dark-adapted, we would find it impossible to read a newspaper – although we might be able to make out the big headlines. However, when we are experiencing a higher illuminance – for instance, when we are in a well-lit room – we adapt to that level, and then can read small print. The smaller the detail we want to see, the higher must be the illuminance provided on the task.

The three main factors that determine our need for light are:

- The apparent size of the detail that we have to see, i.e. the combination of the size of the detail and the distance at which it must be seen. For example, it is more difficult to thread a needle at arm's length than near to our eyes.

- The contrast in reflection factor between the detail to be seen and its background. For example, it is more difficult to thread a needle with dark thread against a dark background than against a light one.

- The duration of the task. For example, one could just manage to thread one needle in a poor light, but it would be very tiring to have to thread needles in a poor light hour after hour. Another important factor is that older eyes need more light to see as well – or nearly as well – as younger eyes.

The *Code for Interior Lighting* published by the Lighting Division of the Chartered Institution of Building Services Engineers gives recommendations for illuminances needed for many kinds of interiors and the tasks to be performed in them. It is important to note that the *Code* recommends that lighting levels should be increased by 50 to 100 per cent in old people's homes, or where the family includes elderly persons. The *Code* also shows that we need about six times more illuminance for performing difficult visual tasks than we need for casual seeing.

The guidelines in Part 1 of this book will enable the homemaker to provide sufficient and suitable lighting for the various rooms and activities discussed. There is a theoretical basis for the recommendations but, in choosing lighting for our home, we do not need to perform calculations, nor do we need to check the illuminance with a lightmeter. Our eyes will tell us if we have achieved a good result.

In typical cases, what proportion of the light output from the lamps actually lights the room?

Some light from a lamp is absorbed within the lighting fitting; some goes directly to illuminate tasks, the table surfaces and the floor; some flows on to the ceiling and upper walls where part is absorbed, and part is reflected usefully towards the tasks, table surfaces, etc. The proportion of the lamp lumens that is usefully employed on the important surfaces is called the *utilisation factor*; typically, this is between one-fifth and three-quarters of the lamp lumens, depending on the type of fittings used and where they are placed in the room.

If the walls, ceiling and other surfaces in the room have pale colours, they will reflect more light, and therefore such a room can be lit with a smaller total wattage of lamps, with a saving in running cost.

Of course, it makes sense to use high-efficacy lamps (such as compact fluorescent lamps, discussed in Chapter 11); but because the total cost of lighting is relatively small compared with other household expenses, we should be more concerned with the appearance of the room than with creating a highly efficient lighting system (as is necessary in offices and factories).

A well-lit room at home is a real pleasure. Choosing lighting fittings that suit your taste and arranging the lighting of the room to achieve a charming appearance is a most satisfying experience. By selecting the most suitable lighting fittings and lamps, it is possible to achieve both the appearance you desire and economy. Don't try to be too scientific, but allow for a generous amount of 'spill light', i.e. light that flows about the room and illuminates its surfaces; such light is not wasted, for it contributes to the pleasant appearance and visual comfort of the interior.

LAMPS

Which types of lamps are most commonly used for domestic lighting?

- *Filament lamps* (bulbs). These are currently the most commonly used type of lamp and provide most of the light we use at home. They are used both for general lighting and local lighting.

- *Compact fluorescent lamps* (CFLs). These are energy-efficient lamps with long lives which come in a variety of shapes. They are used both for general lighting and local lighting.

- *Tubular fluorescent lamps* (tubes). These are mainly used for lighting in kitchens, utility rooms, garages and home workshops.

- *Tungsten-halogen lamps* (TH lamps). These are used in some downlighters, uplighters and wall-washer fittings, and in outdoor floodlights.

- *Reflector lamps* (mushroom lamps). These are filament lamps with an internally silvered reflector bulb, and are used for indoor highlighting and effect lighting. *PAR lamps* are similar to reflector lamps, but have a pressed-glass bulb and, in suitable lighting fittings, are used for garden lighting.

- *Low-voltage tungsten-halogen lamps* (LVTH; dichroic reflector lamps). These are miniature tungsten-halogen lamps in small, very efficient dichroic reflectors. They are used for highlighting and effect lighting.

(Other types of lamps which are clearly unsuitable for lighting homes and gardens, i.e. those used mainly for lighting shops, offices, factories and streets, are not discussed in this book.)

FIGURE 11.1
General construction of a filament lamp.

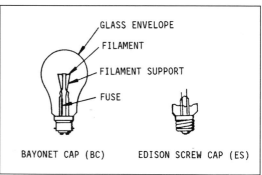

FILAMENT LAMPS

How do filament lamps work?

A filament lamp comprises a fine wire of tungsten metal (the filament) in a glass bulb (the envelope) (see Figure 11.1). The filament is coiled, and may be double-coiled for greater strength and to increase the light output slightly by retaining heat. The envelope contains an inert gas to prevent the filament oxidising and to reduce the tendency for molecules of tungsten to 'boil off' the hot filament and blacken the bulb. The loss of tungsten results in thinning of the filament, eventually causing it to break and so cause the end of its life.

What is the life expectancy of filament lamps?

The rated life of filament lamps is 1,000 hours. This would be the average life of a batch of lamps, some lasting longer and some failing earlier. Shorter life results if filament lamps are mounted cap-down or horizontally. (Note: candle lamps are designed to operate cap-down.) Vibration shortens lamp life; for example, lamps in a pendant fitting in a living room may fail early if subjected to vibration due to children jumping on the floor above.

Is the use of 2,000-hour lamps still warranted?

Lamps are designed to give a balance between the factors of life, efficacy and colour. Improvement of any one of these must be at the cost of the others. Thus filament lamps designed for longer life (e.g. such as 'long-life' and 'double-life' lamps) give lower light output and poorer colour of light than do 1,000-hour lamps.

In the past these lamps have been used where access for relamping was difficult, or to reduce the frequency of lamp failures for the sake of safety. Except in situations where there is frequent switching, their use cannot be justified now that compact fluorescent lamps are available with lives of 5,000 hours or greater. CFLs are also far cheaper to run than any kind of filament lamp.

Filament lamps are available in a range of tinted diffusing envelopes which can be used to impart a gentle colouration to the light. The effect can be very pleasing in bedrooms.

What sizes of filament lamps are used for home lighting?

The powers and lumen outputs of lamps commonly used in the home are as follows:

Watts	25*	40	60	100	150
Lumens (pearl bulbs)	200	390	665	1260	1960

* 25 W lamps are made in singlecoil only; the others have 'coiled-coil' filaments.

In addition to the above, single-ended and double-ended straight 'architectural tubular lamps' are used in some picture lights (see Figure 11.2), and curved and circular lamps of this type are also available.

There are various types of special lamps, such as colour-sprayed lamps, and clear-tinted lamps – for example, the clear 'fire-glow' amber-coloured

RIGHT: Filament lamps with diffusing envelopes such as 'Pearl' (left) and 'Opal' (right) give a slightly diffused light, and are generally preferable to lamps with clear envelopes for home lighting.

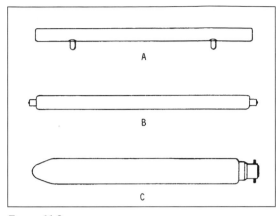

FIGURE 11.2
Some types of architectural lamps.
A: architectural straight lamp with concealed pegs. B: double-ended architectural straight lamp (striplight lamp). C: single-cap straight architectural lamp.

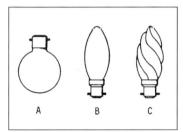

FIGURE 11.3
Some types of decorative lamps. A: 45 mm spherical lamp. B: plain candle lamp. C: twisted candle lamp.

bulb that is used to simulate the warmth of a solid-fuel fire in some electric heaters. Pink, soft-coloured lamps are available, and are often preferred for lighting bedrooms.

Colour-sprayed 5 W pygmy lamps are available, which are suitable as nursery nightlights when used in an appropriate luminaire. (Alternatively a pygmy neon glow lamp can be used in this application.)

Other types of filament lamp used for home lighting include 45 mm diameter spherical lamps, and decorative 'candle lamps' in a variety of sizes, wattages and shapes (including a type that flickers in simulation of a candle flame). Some typical lamps are illustrated in Figure 11.3.

What sort of lampcaps do filament lamps have?

The lamp you use must have a lampcap to suit the lampholder in the luminaire. Most filament lamps used in the home have a 'bayonet cap' (BC) or an 'Edison screw' (ES) cap (see Figure 11.1). Most reflectorised-bulb lamps (i.e. mushroom lamps and PAR lamps) have ES caps to enable them to be firmly and accurately positioned in spotlights. Some luminaires employ types of miniature lamps and decorative lamps with a 'small bayonet cap' (SBC) or 'small Edison screw' (SES) cap.

Why do some filament lamps have smaller bulbs?

Some lampmakers offer filament lamps in conventional or mushroom-shaped envelopes which are slightly smaller than standard lamps. Except where these lamps are specified for use in luminaires of very restricted dimensions, they do not seem to have any particular benefit for the user.

When should 'pearl' or 'clear' filament lamps be used?

Filament lamps may have either clear or diffusing envelopes. Diffusing types are called 'pearl' or 'opal', or may carry a brand-name description. All have the property of concealing the intensely bright filament by diffusion, some presenting a more-or-less uniformly bright envelope. Lamps with diffusing envelopes throw softer shadows, and generally make the lighting rather more pleasant by reducing its harshness, but all give slightly lower lumen outputs than do clear lamps.

Where it is desired to create a brilliant, sparkling effect, as in chandeliers, lamp shapes 'B' and 'C' shown in Figure 11.3 may be used with clear envelopes; but for general use, all filament lamps used in the home should preferably be pearl or opal types.

TUBULAR FLUORESCENT LAMPS

How do tubular fluorescent lamps work?

The following description of the principle of operation of tubular fluorescent lamps applies also to compact fluorescent lamps which are discussed in the following section of this chapter.

Fluorescent lamps consist essentially of a tubular glass envelope containing a low-pressure mercury vapour through which a diffuse electric arc passes (see Figure 11.4). The arc produces a faint blue light which is rich in ultraviolet (UV) light. The UV activates a fluorescent powder coating on the inside of the glass tube, causing it to emit visible light of a colour determined by its chemical composition. Only visible light is transmitted out of the lamp; the UV radiation cannot pass through the glass envelope.

All fluorescent lamps must be operated with some form of control gear to regulate the passage of current through the lamp. This may be 'inductive' (comprising an iron-cored 'choke' and possibly a starter switch) or 'electronic'. Modern electronic control gear operates at high frequency, enabling the lamp to start rapidly and exhibit no visible flicker.

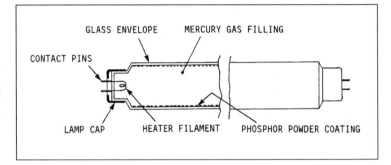

FIGURE 11.4
Construction of a tubular fluorescent lamp.

What types of fluorescent tubular lamps are likely to be most useful in domestic lighting?

The standard diameter of fluorescent lamps was formerly 38 mm (T12 size), but the modern standard is 26 mm diameter (T8 size). Types of T8 lamp are available for retrofit into lighting fittings formerly fitted with T12 lamps.

Fluorescent lamps are available in a wide range of phosphor colours, those giving better colour rendering tending to give slightly lower outputs. The various phosphor colours are not standard between the lampmakers.

Typical domestic lighting requirements for kitchens and all other rooms can be met by using only 'Warm White' lamps. These are designated 'Warm White' by Mazda and Crompton Lighting, 'WW129' by Sylvania, 'Warm White 29' (or Colours 83 or 93) by Philips, and 'Warm White 30' by Osram. The sizes of 26 mm diameter tubular fluorescent lamps most likely to be useful in home lighting applications are the 18 watt (600 mm long) and the 36 watt (1,200 mm long).

For lighting under kitchen cabinets (see Chapters 4 and 14), the lamp of choice is the type 'F8/29' 8 W miniature lamp, 290 mm long by 15 mm in diameter, of 'Warm White' colour.

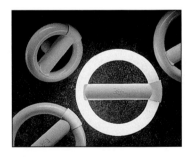

Fluorescent tubular bulbs are available in circular shape, for example the Osram 'Circolux'™ lamps which are made in powers of 18, 24 and 32 watts. Such lamps are used indoors in pendant fittings and dining lights, and in enclosed 'bulkhead' fittings for outdoor use.

COMPACT FLUORESCENT LAMPS

There is a good case for replacing those filament lamps which burn for long hours with retrofit types of compact fluorescent lamps. For example, the Osram Dulux EL lamps have an average life of 8000 hours and can achieve savings in costs of energy and replacement lamps of up to £58 per lamp life.

Note: The principle of operation of compact fluorescent lamps is exactly the same as that given for tubular fluorescent lamps in the preceding section of this chapter.

Will CFLs completely supplant filament lamps?

From time to time, writers on lighting matters report that lamp manufacturers will soon make compact fluorescent lamps even smaller and much cheaper, and they predict that CFLs will shortly entirely supplant the filament lamp, which will become a museum piece. This seems most unlikely for, at present, one cannot make an economic case for using CFLs in lighting fittings that are only used for a few hours per year. More and more homeowners want to be able to dim their lights but, at present, only certain four-pin CFLs (Types PLC, PLL and 2L) can be dimmed. CFL lamps take about a minute to come to full brightness (longer when cold), so they are not suitable for frequent switching outdoors, nor for use in rooms such as toilets where the occupancy is often just a matter of minutes. It therefore seems likely that, for the foreseeable future, we will continue to use a mixture of filament lamps and CFL lamps, as well as other types of lamp where appropriate.

As explained in Chapter 1, using compact fluorescent lamps in situations where the lamp is lit for long hours without frequent switching can result in significant savings. Even though CFLs are more expensive to purchase than filament lamps, adopting them in such situations will result in a worthwhile reduction in your annual expenditure on electricity and replacement lamps.

The construction and operation of compact fluorescent lamps are similar to those of tubular fluorescent lamps which are described in this chapter.

What is meant by 'retrofit' and 'embodiment' types of CFL?

'Retrofit' and 'embodiment' are trade jargon words, but they may help you understand a matter that is confusing to many people. The classifications of 'retrofit' and 'embodiment' are arbitrary, but the essential fact is that there are some types of compact fluorescent lamp that seem to be favoured by manufacturers of lighting fittings, who manufacture special fittings to utilise particular types of CFL which we call 'embodiment' types.

Bearing in mind that the various lampmakers do not all use exactly the same name for each type of compact fluorescent lamp, and remembering also that the lamp designations may be changed, and that new designs of lamps are appearing all the time, we can state that currently you may purchase lighting fittings that embody Type PL-S, Type PL-C or Type PL-L

'Retrofit' compact fluorescent lamps (see previous page) are simple to use, for they may replace existing filament lamps in the same lampholders with immediate energy savings.

single-ended linear lamps (which are of two varieties, two-pin and four-pin). Then there is the Type PL-T lamp (which has three luminous tubes, bent into U-shapes) which is used in certain downlighters designed to take them. All these types of CFL have separate control gear which has to be incorporated into the lighting fitting and wired up. When you buy a lighting fitting containing any of these lamps, it comes to you complete with the lamp, the control gear and any starter switch required, all embodied in it. Having purchased such a fitting, it might be some years before you will need to replace the lamps, when your best strategy would be to take the old lamp to your lighting supplier and ask them to supply a replacement.

The second class of CFL, which we term 'retrofit' types, are those that, increasingly, you will find stocked in the lighting shops. These are lamps that can be purchased by the home owner, and just popped into lampholders that were previously occupied by filament lamps. Again remembering that new types of CFL seem to be appearing all the time, we can identify the following types as suitable for retrofitting into your existing lighting

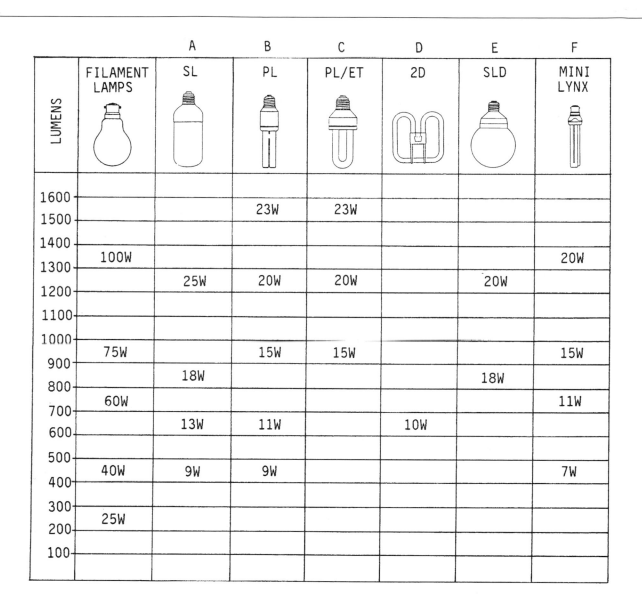

FIGURE 11.5
A table showing the approximate comparative light outputs of six popular types of compact fluorescent lamps which are suitable for retrofit into existing lighting fittings to replace filament lamps.

fittings or for installing into new fittings that you may buy: Types SL, PL Electronic, PL/ET Electronic, 2D, SL Electronic, SLD Electronic and Mini-Lynx (see Figure 11.5).

Most of the lamps in this 'retrofit' class are available with either BC or ES lampcaps, but some retailers may not stock the BC versions. Because CFLs are heavier than filament lamps, they can tend to mount crookedly in a

BC lampholder; therefore, if you are going to change over to CFLs, it would be preferable – but not essential – to replace the BC lampholders in your lighting fittings with ES lampholders. The screw action of an ES lampholder ensures a good electrical contact, especially if the lamp is mounted horizontally.

What are the characteristics of the popular 'retrofit' types of compact fluorescent lamp?

Most people have some idea of how much light is given by the familiar sizes of filament lamps, so in Figure 11.5 we use the light outputs of filament lamps as the basis for comparison with the typical light outputs of six selected types of CFL. The table is only a guide; to ascertain the actual lumen outputs, refer to the lampmakers' literature.

The six types of compact fluorescent lamp listed in Figure 11.5 and described below may be simply plugged into your existing lighting fittings to replace the filament lamps. It is important to note that none of these lamps is suitable for use on dimming circuits. Also, when inserting these lamps into existing lighting fittings, remember that they are of different shape and size to the filament lamps they replace, and that not all your existing lighting fittings may be suitable to receive them. In particular, note that the lampshades used on portable lighting fittings may need to be replaced with larger ones to avoid unnecessarily trapping a lot of light. In general, large cylindrical rather small cone-shaped shades are best.

Compact fluorescent lamps, such as this Type PL lamp, present no technical problems for the user. Just place it in the lampholder, and switch on.

• *Type SL lamp* (see A in Figure 11.5). This is a useful and versatile type of lamp, suitable to use in general lighting fittings and in local lighting fittings. It is intended for normal indoor use, but is widely used outdoors in 'jam-jar' lighting fittings and other weatherproof types of fitting for domestic security lighting. The light output is lower when the lamp is cold. Lamp life is 8,000 hours on average. Type SL lamps come in powers of 9 watts, 13 watts, 18 watts and 25 watts, and have envelopes that are either 'prismatic' or 'diffusing'. BC and ES caps are available. The control gear is inside the lamp and is therefore discarded with the lamp at the end of lamp life.

• *Type PL Electronic lamp* (see B in Figure 11.5). This type of lamp has four luminous 'legs' (actually two loops) and is suitable for general lighting and local lighting, and for external use in suitable lighting fittings. It is suitable for use in any operating position, e.g. cap-up, cap-down or horizontal. Its light output is lower when cold. Lamp life is 8,000 hours on average. Type PL Electronic lamps come in powers of 9 watts, 11 watts, 15 watts and 23 watts. BC and ES cap versions are available. The control gear is attached to the end of the lamp and is discarded with the lamp at the end of lamp life.

- *Type PL/ET Electronic lamp* (see C in Figure 11.5). This type of lamp has three U-shaped luminous tubes and is suitable for general lighting and local lighting, and for external use in suitable lighting fittings. It is suitable for use in any operating position, e.g. cap-up, cap-down or horizontal. Incorporating high-frequency electronic control gear, it gives fast starting and no discernible flicker, and has improved cold-starting performance. Type PL Electronic lamps come in powers of 9 watts, 11 watts, 15 watts and 23 watts. BC and ES cap versions are available. The control gear is attached to the end of the lamp and is discarded with the lamp at the end of lamp life.

- *Type 2D lamp* (see D in Figure 11.5). This type of lamp has two D-shaped luminous tubes in a flat configuration. It is suitable for general lighting and local lighting, and for external use in suitable lighting fittings. It is suitable for use in any operating position. Lamp life is 8,000 hours on average. The retrofit Type 2D lamp comes only in a power of 10 watts plus the control gear losses, i.e. the inductive form of control gear adaptor consumes 4 watts, while the electronic version of control gear consumes 3 watts.

The 10-watt Type '2D' (tm) lamp has a separate (reusable) control gear which is placed in the lampholder first, and then the lamp is inserted into that.

The control gear unit has a lampcap (BC or ES for the inductive pattern of control gear, BC only for the electronic pattern); this lampcap is inserted into the lampholder of a lighting fitting, and then the lamp is plugged into the control gear. At the end of lamp life, the lamp is discarded, but the control gear can be retained for further use. The control gear has a life of 32,000 hours, i.e. it will last through four lamp lives. (Other patterns of this type of lamp which are not suitable for retrofit are used in a number of purpose-made lighting fittings, including exterior bulkhead fittings suitable for mounting flat to a wall or ceiling.)

- Types SL and SLD lamps (see E in Figure 11.5). These have spherical opal envelopes of 115 mm and 121 mm diameter respectively. They can be used in any position if adequately supported. Being of light weight they may be used in 'rise-and-fall' dining-table lamps. Type SL lamps are of 18 W rating. Type SLD are rated at 20 watts and incorporate electronic control gear which gives fast starting and freedom from flicker even at low temperatures. In both types, the control gear is within the lamp and is discarded with the lamp at the end of lamp life.

- *Mini-Lynx (tm) lamps* (see F in Figure 11.5). These lamps have four luminous 'arms' (two U-shaped tubes) with integral control gear and are provided with an ES or BC cap. Life is 8,000 hours on average. The ratings available are 7 watts, 11 watts, 15 watts and 20 watts. Lengths range between 120 mm and 207 mm according to power and whether the type of control gear incorporated into the lamp is inductive or electronic. At the end of lamp life, the complete lamp including its integral control gear is discarded.

TUNGSTEN-HALOGEN LAMPS

How do tungsten-halogen (TH) lamps work?

Tungsten-halogen lamps are used in domestic uplighters, and in wall-washer fittings. They are also the source of choice for small external floodlights (see Chapters 8 and 15).

Tungsten-halogen (TH) lamps are a form of filament lamp in which the coiled filament is mounted in a narrow tubular envelope of fused silica (quartz) (see Figure 11.6). The gas filling of the envelope contains a halogen gas (iodine or bromine, etc.), which has the property of combining with tungsten in certain conditions. When the tungsten mole-

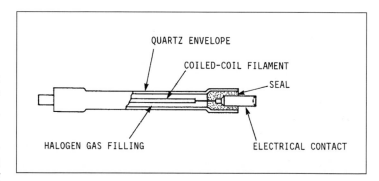

**FIGURE 11.6
Construction of a linear tungsten-halogen lamp.**

cules 'boil off' the filament, they are captured by the halogen molecules. The halogen molecules have an affinity for tungsten, and so are attracted back to the filament and thus help to prevent it thinning. But at filament temperature, the tungsten-halogen molecules break up, and the halogen returns to the gas filling to await the capture of another tungsten molecule – thus completing the 'halogen cycle'. If it could be arranged that the tungsten molecules replaced themselves evenly on the filament, the filament would never thin and the lamp would last forever! In practice, the halogen cycle extends the lamp life to 2,000 hours, twice that of ordinary filament lamps. Because the filament in a tungsten-halogen lamp operates at a higher temperature than that of other filament lamps, the lamp has a higher efficacy, and produces whiter (bluer) light. Lamp powers of 200 watts and 300 watts are used in wall-washers; the 200 W, 300 W and 500 W sizes are used for garden floodlighting.

It is important never to touch the quartz envelope of a tungsten-halogen lamp with your bare hand, for fats from your skin may migrate into the quartz and cause early failure of the lamp.

Caution: Do not touch a tungsten-halogen lamp soon after its failure or soon after switching it off, for it remains very hot for some time.

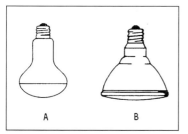

FIGURE 11.7
Popular types of reflector lamps.
A: blown-glass reflector lamp.
B: PAR lamp.

REFLECTOR LAMPS AND PAR LAMPS

What types of reflector lamp are available?

Two types of reflector lamp are useful in domestic lighting: blown-glass reflector lamps (popularly known as 'mushroom lamps') and PAR lamps (see Figure 11.7). (Crown-silvered reflector lamps which are used in parabolic reflectors are still available, but are being superseded by low-voltage tungsten-halogen lamps.)

A *mushroom lamp* is a filament lamp with a blown-glass internally silvered reflector envelope. This type of lamp is made in three physical sizes: 50 mm diameter (25 watts and 40 watts), 63 mm diameter (40 watts and 60 watts) and 80 mm diameter (40 watts, 60 watts, 75 watts and 100 watts). Reflector lamps are available with clear bulbs, or blue, red, green, yellow or amber bulbs.

When purchasing a reflector lamp, ensure that you choose a lamp of the correct diameter for your lighting fitting. An oversize lamp will restrict air movement in the fitting, which may overheat.

A 'Gro-Lux' (tm) spotlamp is available. This is a 75 W reflector lamp with a special internal reflector coating which reflects infra-red as well as visible light, and is used in the cultivation of plants in the greenhouse or indoors.

PAR lamps are similar to mushroom lamps except that they are housed in a robust pressed-glass envelope with ES cap. The common size is the PAR 38 (120 mm diameter) which is available in powers of 60 watts, 80 watts and 120 watts with clear glasses. Eighty-watt PAR 38 lamps are available with clear, blue, green, red or yellow bulbs, and are used in spike lamps for decorative garden lighting.

LOW-VOLTAGE TUNGSTEN-HALOGEN LAMPS

Low-voltage tungsten-halogen (LVTH) lamps provide an attractive and convenient means of spotlighting and emphasis lighting in the home. Their principle of operation is the same as that described earlier for mains-voltage tungsten-halogen lamps. The filament in an LVTH lamp operates at a higher temperature than that of ordinary filament lamps, and hence produces a whiter, bluer light. LVTH lamps have higher efficacy than ordinary filament lamps, and an average life of 2,000 hours.

LVTH 'capsule lamps' are used in some modern downlighters and spotlight fittings, and these give sharp beam definition. Capsule lamps are also employed in some desklamps.

Warning: Unless it is fitted with an ultraviolet-light filter, continuous exposure of the skin at close range to the light from an LVTH lamp in a desk lamp could be dangerous.

It is possible to dim LVTH lamps but, if the temperature of the lamp is reduced below a certain point, the 'halogen cycle' will not operate and the lamp will start to blacken. Restoring the lamp to normal power should remove the blackening; if it is not restored to normal power, early failure of the lamp will result.

Miniature LVTH lamps with 30 mm or 50 mm diameter dichroic reflectors are widely used in spotlights of various patterns and on lighting track (see Figure 11.8). These intensely bright small lamps are made in powers of 20 watts, 35 watts and 50 watts, in narrow-, medium- and wide-beam angles. The filament in such lamps may be mounted transversely in the reflector, or axially; the latter is preferred as it tends to produce a more evenly bright patch of light. *Warning:* Remember that these small lamps are intensely hot and should not be touched, and that their beams are hot enough to ignite flammable materials at close proximity.

The preferred types of miniature LVTH reflector lamps have a clear heat-resisting glass cover over the reflector. If the quartz capsule were to shatter

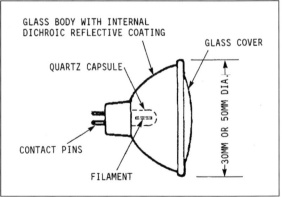

FIGURE 11.8
Construction of a low-voltage tungsten-halogen (LVTH) lamp.

while the lamp was lit, the glass cover would reduce the risk of injury or fire by preventing hot fragments falling from the lamp.

The 12 V supply for LVTH lamps has to be derived either from a *step-down transformer* or from an *electronic voltage reducer*. A group of lamps may be supplied from one such unit – for example, lamps mounted on a length of lighting track. The total wattage of the lamps connected to any 12 V supply must not exceed the power capacity of the unit, or its voltage may be reduced, and this could shorten the life of the lamps if they do not operate at a temperature high enough to ensure that the halogen cycle functions.

It is important to replace promptly any failed lamps in a group sharing a common 12 V supply for, on failure of the first lamp, the voltage applied to the remaining lamps tends to rise, and this is likely to cause their early failure. This effect is more likely to occur with step-down transformers than with electronic voltage reducers which generally have better 'voltage regulation'.

Choosing
LIGHTING FITTINGS
for YOUR HOME

What are the principal features of the types of lighting fitting used in the home?

Lighting fittings come in a wide variety of shapes and constructions, ranging from utilitarian devices such as weatherproof bulkhead fittings for outdoor use, to artistic and beautiful decorative shades for portable lamps in both modern and traditional designs.

A shaded bedside lamp and a scintillating crystal chandelier may not appear to have much in common but, like all lighting fittings, they both perform the same basic functions of housing and supporting one or more lamps and providing the means of safely connecting them to the electrical supply. Permanently installed lighting fittings have some means of attachment to the wall or ceiling; portable lighting fittings other than hand lamps have a base so that the fitting can stand on the floor or a table. Lighting fittings for fluorescent tubular lamps contain the lamp control gear and possibly a starter switch. Some lighting fittings have a built-in switch or dimmer. According to its purpose, a lighting fitting will have means of controlling the flow of light from the lamp by means of a reflector, a shade or a diffuser.

How should one choose portable lighting fittings and shades?

Many lighting fittings for the home are purchased on impulse. One may see a fitting in a display, or as part of an attractive room setting, and immediately visualise it as being just what you need to brighten up a certain spot at home. It may be that when you get the new fitting home it becomes apparent that it really does not suit the room in some way, or that the new fitting looks out of place against the colours or style of your decor. Worse, when installed, the new fitting may give light of an unsuitable character in the chosen position.

In choosing lighting fittings for the home, personal preferences are

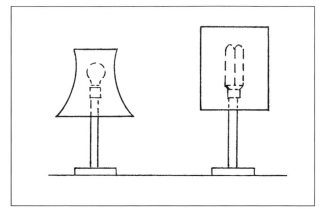

FIGURE 12.1 CHANGING TO CFL LAMPS
A table lamp with a small shade
(left) could employ a compact fluorescent lamp, but most of the light
would be trapped within the shade.
It would be better to change to a
larger shade with a larger top
aperture (right).

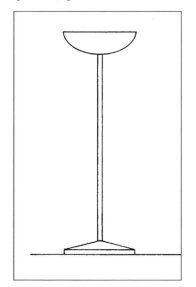

FIGURE 12.2 A TYPICAL UPLIGHTER
An uplighter containing a 300W or
500W tungsten-halogen lamp will
probably make an overbright patch
on the ceiling if the ceiling height is
low. In homes with low ceilings, an
uplighter containing one or two
compact fluorescent lamps will
probably be much more suitable.

important; all the expert advice in the world will not convince you that something looks good if you think it is ugly. So here are a few guidelines which can help prevent disappointments.

Portable lighting fittings, especially small decorative table lamps, may be purchased more for their appearance as charming objects than for their lighting function. While some variation in style is acceptable, a lighting fitting that blatantly clashes with the style, period or colour of a room's decor could be rather irritating. (That is one of the problems of buying a lighting fitting as a present for someone else!)

When choosing lampshades for table lamps and floor standard lamps for your own home, it is generally not too difficult to select lampshades of suitable size and shape; but finding the one that you like in a colour that suits your room can be quite a problem. When you go shopping, it is a good idea to have some colour samples with you – perhaps snippets of the materials used for your curtains or furnishing fabrics – so you can ensure that the shades you choose will not clash with your room colours.

You might like to try making up your own lampshades. Some departmental stores and lighting retailers sell the wire frames for lampshades for you to cover them in a material of your choice, and provide a cutting pattern and instructions. When buying the covering material, don't forget to buy a piece of suitable white material with which to line the lampshade, or it will give out very little light.

In many homes you will find tiny table lamps which are more for decoration than for lighting, and which are fitted with very small shades, just big enough to house a low-power filament lamp. If you are thinking of putting compact fluorescent lamps in these, do remember that CFLs are generally rather bigger than filament lamps. For example, if you want to use one of the six types of 'retrofit' CFLs identified in Figure 11.5, you should choose a shade that is deep enough to conceal the CFL lamp completely, and preferably one that is rather more cylindrical than cone-shaped – so that it lets light out at the top.

What are the considerations when choosing an uplighter?

If you are going out to buy any kind of lighting fittings, it is well worth while taking with you a note of the rough dimensions of your room – especially the ceiling height. This is important if you are thinking of buying an uplighter. Uplighters are usually a little under 2 m tall (higher than the eye level of a tall person) so that the bright lamp in it cannot be seen. If you happen to live in a house that has low ceilings, and the uplighter you choose has, say, a 300 W tungsten-halogen lamp, unless it has a really efficient wide-spreading reflector, it could create a rather uncomfortably bright patch on the ceiling.

For rooms with a moderate to low ceiling height, an uplighter designed to house one or two compact fluorescent lamps is more likely to create the lighting effect that you have in mind, i.e. a pleasant, broad, soft-edged spread of light on the ceiling which is reflected back to produce a gentle glow of general lighting across the whole room. Perhaps the retailer will demonstrate the uplighter to you at the correct distance below a flat, non-shiny white ceiling so that you can judge the effect.

A well-made uplighter will have a heavy base and will not be easily tipped over. But do remember that it will probably be standing on a carpet at home, and therefore not quite so stable as it seems when demonstrated to you as it will be standing on a hard floor in the shop. It is recommended that all free-standing uplighters should be fitted in manufacture with a *tilt switch* which isolates the lamp from the supply if the uplighter is tilted beyond a safe angle. This is important if you purchase an uplighter containing a tungsten-halogen lamp, and particularly so if you have young children at home.

What about the flexible lead and fused plug for a new portable lighting fitting?

Before going out to buy a portable lighting fitting, measure the run between the nearest socket outlet and the place where you want the fitting to stand, and remember to take your tape measure with you. In the shop, check the length of the lead provided with the fitting, and ask the retailer to fit a longer one if necessary. Most lighting retailers will be glad to do this and also to fit a 3-pin plug-top containing the correct size of fuse.

It is regrettable that many portable lighting fittings which are sold complete with lead and plug have a 13 A fuse in the plug – which is much too big and gives little protection. If the fuse size has not been checked by the retailer, before you plug in, check the size of the fuse in the plug-top. The usual size of fuse for a portable lighting fitting is *3 amperes* – which will suit a load of up to 690 watts.

If you are thinking of buying additional spotlights, downlighters, etc., to fit on a ceiling lighting track that is already installed at home, take the exact details of the track system with you – for example, you could take the instruction leaflet supplied with the track. There are many patterns of lighting track, and the fitments for them are not all interchangeable.

How can one ensure that lighting fittings that one buys are safe and of good quality?

Your search should be for quality as well as style. Companies that have a quality system conforming to BS 5750 and are assessed as such by the British Standards Institution may display the BSI symbol on their literature.

Seek lighting fittings that display the BSI Kitemark or BSI Safety Mark to indicate independent testing of samples to BS 4533 and assessment of production procedures to BS 5750 by the BSI.

Metallic lighting fittings such as desk lamps, directable spotlamps, etc., should be marked 'double insulated', or they should have an earth connection and be fitted with a three-core flexible lead.

It is worth bearing in mind that many reputable British lighting manufacturers and lighting retailers are members of The Lighting Association or The Lighting Industry Federation, both of which organisations give leadership and standards to their members in respect of the quality and safety of the lighting products they offer.

DIMMING

What is the value of dimmers in home lighting?

Dimming, of both permanently installed lighting and portable lighting, can be an elegant improvement to home lighting, enabling you to match the lighting level to the mood and needs of the moment in the living room (see Chapter 3) and in the bedroom (see Chapter 5). In the living room on a dull day, if one is using the electric lighting to augment available daylight, the lighting level can be raised. During the evening, the lights can be turned low to change the room appearance completely. In the bedroom, dimmed lighting is reassuring to a sick or sleepless person or to a restless child.

Derek Phillips, architect and well-known expert on lighting, writing in the magazine *Lighting Equipment News* (January 1994), says, 'I believe that dimmers have a role to play in home lighting, the best being those which provide a number of "scenesets" – but simple dimmers can also play a part.' He goes on to say, 'Dimmers allow a change of mood to take account of the different activities in the modern home. The sitting room is used for watching television, conversation, needlework, homework, parties and so forth; no one level of light from the various light fittings can provide for this.'

Can all kinds of lamp be operated on dimmers?

No; it is not practicable to dim the current types of compact fluorescent lamps other than those with four-pin lamp connectors (e.g. Types PLL and 2L) for which appropriate dimmers may be available. With suitable dimmers, these, and tubular fluorescent lamps operated with high-frequency control gear, can be dimmed down to extinction; but some dimmers for fluorescent lamps operating with inductive control gear cannot dim the lamp to lower than about 15 per cent of its full light output.

The control panel (on the left of the picture) enables a range of 'scene-sets' to be selected, the lamps brightening or dimming to programmed chosen values.

Does dimming a lamp save energy?

Yes; but in some cases the electrical losses in the dimmer circuit may cancel out the reduction in energy used by the lamp. However, dimming filament lamps generally results in a worthwhile saving; for example, dimming a filament lamp to 50 per cent of its normal light output will reduce the energy consumption by 40 per cent.

Will the life of lamps be extended if they are operated on dimmers?

Generally, yes. The effect is most marked in the case of filament lamps. For example, dimming a filament lamp to 50 per cent of light output will extend the life of the lamp by a factor of 20. Dimming tungsten-halogen lamps theoretically extends lamp life, but if the lamp is operated below a certain temperature, the 'halogen cycle' does not occur, and the lamp will blacken and fail prematurely if operated at that reduced voltage for a long period.

Does dimming affect the colour of the light from the lamp?

In the case of fluorescent lamps there is no change in the colour of the light output. The light emitted by filament lamps as they are dimmed becomes progressively 'warmer', i.e. pinker.

How do lighting dimmers work?

The modern solid-state dimmer is one of the many products that have become practicable and cheap since miniature electronic devices became available. A dimmer 'slices' the current into incredibly brief pulses, the frequency and amplitude of which are varied to control the power delivered to the lamp and hence to control the lamp's light output.

Select your dimmer to match the type of lamp and the load (the total wattage of lamps to be controlled by the dimmer).

Can lighting equipment and dimmers cause radio interference?

Manufacturers of lighting equipment and dimmers are required by law to provide basic suppression of the radio frequency interference (RFI) emitted by such equipment. However, if the dimmer device, the lamp or its flexible cable is placed very close to a radio, television or telephone, etc., or close to the flexible cables connecting them, some interference may occur.

Can dimmers cause audible hum?

Yes. Some dimmers used to control filament lamps and installed in wall-mounted switchboxes can emit an annoying hum, particularly if there is any looseness in the fixings (see Chapter 14). The noise is usually loudest when the dimmer is turned to a low setting. Check that the device is not overloaded. Placing too great a load on the dimmer can cause its early failure. If, after checking the fixings and connections, the dimmer still causes an annoying degree of audible hum, ask the supplier to exchange it.

What types of dimmer controls are available?

Dimmers for circuits containing only filament lamps are available in the form of control units which replace the wall switch. These are not suitable for dimming fluorescent lamps or CFLs. The wall-mounted controller has a knob or slider which is operated to adjust the light output of the lamps, or a touch-plate which on being touched will cause the dimmer circuit to cycle through its range of light output (see Chapter 14).

Such dimmers, and more sophisticated dimmer systems which control a number of lamps in a room, bringing them to several programmed outputs or 'scenesets', are available from specialist manufacturers such as Helvar. On selecting a particular sceneset, some lamps will be dimmed and others brightened to preset values. Thus, the mood of all the lighting in the room can be adjusted to a chosen sceneset by operating a single control.

Dimmers for fluorescent lamps usually consist of two units, a dimmer circuit unit (which may be mounted within the lighting fitting or separately) and a control unit.

Dimmers are also incorporated into individual portable lighting fittings such as table lamps which house a filament lamp and are suitable for use as bedside lamps (see Chapter 5). The built-in dimmer is operated by a knob on the lamp base. Some patterns of desk lamps, housing a small tungsten-halogen lamp, have integral dimmer control.

Also available are 'in-line dimmers' which may be connected into the lead of a portable lighting fitting containing a filament lamp.

Another pattern of dimmer consists of a small unit which fits into the BC or ES lampholder of a portable lighting fitting, and has a lampholder to receive the lamp. The dimmer is adjusted by a small knob on its side.

Caution: A dimmer must only be used with the type of lamp for which it is designed. Do not attempt to use any type of fluorescent lamp on a dimmer designed for filament lamps. Comply with the maker's instructions regarding power and current loadings, and do not fit a lamp of greater wattage than the rated wattage of the dimmer. Read the manufacturer's instructions regarding installation and use, and follow them carefully. In particular, note that the six types of 'retrofit' compact fluorescent lamps identified in Chapter 11 as being suitable for replacing filament lamps must not be used on dimming circuits.

Installing INTERIOR LIGHTING

What should be noted when receiving or unpacking lighting fittings?

Open the packages with care so as not to damage the contents or lose small items such as packets of fixing screws or instruction leaflets. Some lighting manufacturers supply special fixings such as toggle bolts with their lighting fittings.

Do not destroy cartons for, in some cases, installation instructions are printed on the carton or inside the lid, or the carton is printed or perforated to serve as a fixing template.

If lamps are packed with the fittings, read the markings on the lamps to check them for type, voltage, power, colour, etc., before using them.

If there are shortages, or if damage is seen or suspected, notify the carriers and suppliers without delay.

How should lighting equipment be stored before use?

Most interior lighting fittings intended for home use are painted or otherwise treated to resist rust and corrosion in normal home interior conditions. However, they are not protected against the continued effect of damp, and therefore should be stored in a dry, normally heated room until it is desired to utilise them.

What essential precautions must be taken before making any alterations to electric wiring?

If the reader is not trained and experienced in electrical installation work, it is not the intention of this book to encourage him or her to undertake any but the simplest tasks in wiring, such as connecting a ceiling-mounted or pendant lighting fitting or a length of lighting track to an existing ceiling outlet, or installing dimmers into existing switchboxes. If the task lies outside the knowledge and experience of the reader, it is advised that help should be obtained from a properly qualified electrician.

When you intend to open any electrical enclosure (e.g. a ceiling rose or a switchbox) to adjust the wiring, the circuit must be isolated as a protection against electric shock. This may be achieved by opening the main switch or tripping the main circuit-breaker. However, it is not necessary to switch off all the supplies in the house while working on only one circuit; instead, the circuit can be isolated by switching off the circuit switch (the switch that controls the ring-main circuit, for example), or by removing the circuit fuse, or by tripping the MCB for that circuit. Having done this, double-check that the circuit is isolated by switching on a light or appliance and confirming that it does not come on.

Circuits that are fed from a socket outlet can be isolated by opening the switch on the socket outlet and then withdrawing the plug.

At completion of the work, before restoring the supply, check that all connections are correctly made and that the terminal screws are tight. Check also that earth conductors have been properly connected, and that the fixing-cover screws are tight.

How does one wire up a 13 A three-pin plug?

The standard three-pin plug-and-socket system used in the UK is covered by BS 1363. The pins of the plugs are rectangular, and each plug-top contains a cartridge fuse.

It is becoming the practice for portable lighting fittings to be sold complete with a flexible cable and a moulded-on three-pin plug. However, some lighting fittings are of 'double-insulated' construction and do not need an earth wire, but they may still be used with standard three-pin plugs. If such a lighting fitting has a two-core flexible cable and the cores are not colour coded, connect one lead to 'L' (LINE) and the other to 'N' (NEUTRAL).

Some modern three-pin plugs have plastic grips to hold the cable ends within the plug; if the plug you have is of that type, follow the maker's instructions for fitting the three-core flexible lead.

In the case of three-pin plugs having screw terminals to hold the cable ends, to fit a plug to a three-core flexible cable, refer to Figure 14.1 and follow this procedure:

1. With the square pins facing upward, undo the large screw in the centre of the back, and remove the cover.

2. Remove the cartridge fuse. Loosen the three terminal screws.

3. Loosen one of the two screws that retain the cord-grip, and remove the other one. Swing the cord-grip to one side.

4. Strip back the outer sheath of the three-core flexible cable by 50 mm to expose the three cores. (If using a flexible cable that has a fabric braid cover, bind the frayed end of the braid with insulating tape.)

5. Place the flexible cable under the cord-grip as shown in the diagram, and clamp the cable under the cord-grip by tightening the two screws. Check that the flexible cable is held firmly by the cord-grip.

6. Lay the three cores in the plug to see how long each of them should be to fit neatly into the terminals without strain or excessively big loops. Carefully note that:

   (a) the GREEN/YELLOW striped core goes to the 'E' (EARTH) terminal;

   (b) the BROWN core goes to the 'L' (LINE) terminal; and

   (c) the BLUE (NEUTRAL) core goes the the 'N' (NEUTRAL) terminal.

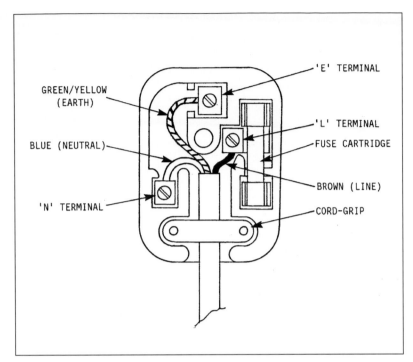

Cut the three cores to appropriate lengths, allowing for each core to enter its terminal by a distance of about 8 mm.

7. Strip 8 mm of insulation from each core, and neaten up the ends by twisting them with your fingers.

8. Insert the stripped core ends into the appropriate terminals, and tighten the terminal screws firmly.

9. Insert the correct size of cartridge fuse into the fuse-holder (see Chapter 9 regarding fuse sizes).

10. Check carefully to ensure that you have connected the three cores correctly.

11. Fit the cover to the plug-top, and secure it with the large screw.

FIGURE 14.1
Interior of a 13 A three-pin plug. Follow the instructions given in Chapter 14 to ensure that you make the connections correctly.

How can additional socket outlets be provided for portable lighting fittings without changing the fixed wiring?

If your house or flat has a reasonable number of three-pin 13 A socket outlets in convenient positions, all that is required to install portable lighting fittings is to connect three-pin plugs to their flexible leads and insert them into nearby socket outlets.

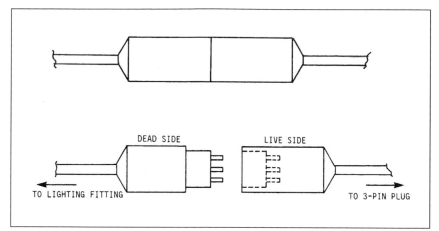

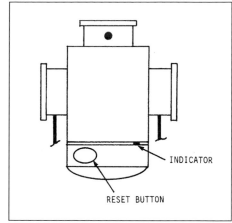

FIGURE 14.2
A typical three-pin line connector which may be used to connect the lead from a lighting fitting to another length of three-core flexible cable in order to extend it.

FIGURE 14.3
Sketch of a three-way socket adaptor fitted with overload protection, an audible alarm and an indicator.

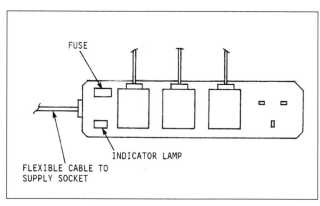

FIGURE 14.4
A multiple trailing socket unit which can provide supplies to several portable lighting fittings at a distance from the only available three-pin socket outlet.

If the distance between the socket outlet and the desired position of the portable lighting fitting is greater than the length of its flexible lead, you could replace the lead with a longer one, or extend it by use of a one-way *trailing socket unit*. Alternatively, a three-pin *line connector* could be used to connect the lead from the lighting fitting to another length of three-core flexible cable (see Figure 14.2).

If it is desired to connect more than one portable lighting fitting to a single three-pin socket outlet, do not attempt to cram the tails of both flexes into one plug, but use two plugs and a two-way or three-way *socket adaptor* at the socket outlet (see Figure 14.3). The adaptor used could be one that is fitted with overload protection; such units are designed to cut off the power and sound an alarm buzzer when overloaded, and are claimed to reduce the risk of electrical fire.

If it is desired to site several portable lighting fittings at a distance from the only available three-pin socket outlet, a single or multiple *trailing socket unit* could be used (see Figure 14.4). Alternatively, it is possible to install some additional wall-mounted socket outlets without recourse to making connections directly to the permanent wiring as explained in the following answer.

How may one install additional wall-mounted socket outlets without altering the permanent wiring?

Quite apart from the possible need to have additional socket outlets for portable lighting fittings, with the increasing use in our homes of electronic entertainment, home computers and electrical appliances, even modern homes may not have enough socket outlets, particularly in the living room or lounge. Typically there is a single or double socket outlet on either side of the fireplace, and these can be quite insufficient if you desire to introduce lighting features on the other side of the room.

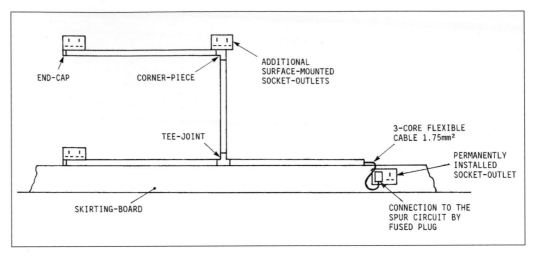

END-CAP   CORNER-PIECE   ADDITIONAL SURFACE-MOUNTED SOCKET-OUTLETS

TEE-JOINT

3-CORE FLEXIBLE CABLE 1.75mm²

PERMANENTLY INSTALLED SOCKET-OUTLET

SKIRTING-BOARD

CONNECTION TO THE SPUR CIRCUIT BY FUSED PLUG

FIGURE 14.5
Additional surface-mounted socket outlets installed with the use of mini-trunking. Connection to the permanent wiring is made by a fused plug inserted in a permanent socket outlet.

One could have additional socket outlets installed by a properly qualified electrician. If one does not wish to install the extra socket outlets permanently, and if some surface runs of very neat white plastic *mini-trunking* would be acceptable, then additional and conveniently located socket outlets can be easily and safely installed by a competent DIYer. The idea is to carry the wiring to the new surface-mounted socket outlets within runs of the mini-trunking along the skirting board as shown in Figure 14.5. This can be done without interfering with the permanent wiring.

The additional socket outlets do not have to be located at skirting-board level. Indeed, if you have an elderly person or a back-sufferer in your household, it may be far more convenient to mount the socket outlets at, say, 700 mm to 1 m above the floor.

The idea is to create a 'spur' off the installed ring-main, by terminating the mini-trunking near one of the permanently installed socket outlets, and to take a supply through a standard fused plug-top to feed the socket outlets along the new mini-trunking. It is important that the total loading on the new spur circuit should not exceed the capacity of the cable and of the fuse in the plug-top by which the new trunking wiring is connected to the permanent socket outlet.

The installation may be made in the following manner. Referring to Figure 14.5, install runs of 16 mm x 16 mm or 1 inch x ½ inch mini-trunking along the chosen route, positioning multipurpose two-gang boxes for the socket outlets at the selected positions. (A complete range of mini-trunking components including corner pieces, capping, two-gang boxes, etc., is available through your electrical supplier.) The mini-trunking should terminate near an existing socket outlet as shown in Figure 14.5, and a standard three-pin fused plug used to connect the new wiring to the existing socket outlet.

Wiring to the new socket outlets must be in a three-core flexible cable of 1.75 sq. mm size, which will ensure that it is large enough to carry the maximum load (13 amperes) that may be plugged into the new socket outlets. This will require the use of mini-trunking of 1 inch x ½ inch in size.

However, if the cable in the mini-trunking run goes straight to a lighting fitting (or, for example, to a cove light or pelmet light) and does not connect to any socket outlets into which any other load could be plugged, then the cable used may be a three-core flexible cable of 0.75 sq. mm size, and the mini-trunking may be of 16 mm x 16 mm size.

The fuse in the three-pin plug which connects the new spur wiring to the permanently installed socket outlet should be of a size suitable for the load, i.e. for direct connection to a lighting load only without any additional socket outlets being fitted, a 3 A fuse should be used.

How are lighting fittings fixed to the ceiling?

Pendant lighting fittings may be supplied with a ceiling plate for fixing directly to an existing ceiling box with the existing screws. The flexible suspension cable for a pendant fitting must be held by a cable-grip within the ceiling rose. *Important:* A lighting fitting must not be suspended by the wire cores of its flexible cable.

The supply cable to a new ceiling point in a top-floor room may be laid in the loft. For downstairs rooms, the supply cable must be introduced into the cavity between the ceiling and the floor above. In houses of traditional construction, ceiling roses should be attached to a timber joist. Locate the joists by tapping the ceiling and noting where a dull sound indicates the joist position. The joist position can be confirmed by probing with a thin bradawl.

Woodscrews fixing ceiling roses should penetrate the joist by at least 20 mm. (The plaster or plasterboard of the ceiling may be between 5 mm and 15 mm thick.)

If there is no joist at the chosen position for a new ceiling rose, or for fixing a lighting fitting directly to the ceiling (for example, for several fixings for a long fluorescent fitting, or for a length of lighting track) *toggle bolts* (also known as butterfly bolts) must be used to fix to a plasterboard or lath-and-plaster ceiling. These have two spring-loaded wings which open after the stem of the bolt has been pushed through the hole in the ceiling, the wings supporting the weight of the lighting fitting on the upper surface of the ceiling material.

If you are proposing to install a new pendant fitting or wall-mounted fitting, consider using plug-in ceiling roses and wall-bracket connectors which are described in Chapter 2. Then it will be a matter of moments to take down any fitting or reinstall it, without have to touch the wiring connections.

How can the hum from fluorescent-lamp fittings be minimised?

Because of the magnetic effect when alternating current is flowing in the control gear, it can produce a low humming noise at twice the mains frequency, i.e. 100 cycles/second. Better-quality control gear tends to produce less hum. Because of variations in production, some control gears tend to be more noisy. 'High-frequency' control gear is inherently quieter, and should be chosen for preference if available.

Hum may be amplified by part of the lighting fitting vibrating in resonance with the frequency of the hum. Loose fixing screws or small items such as washers lying in the fitting or in the diffuser may also create noise.

Tightening screws and ensuring that there are no loose-fitting parts may reduce the nuisance. Hum will be less if the fitting is attached firmly to a solid wall with suitable wall plugs, or, if ceiling mounted, attached to a joist rather than to the ceiling material.

The hum from a lighting fitting controlled by a dimmer may be greater or less when the dimmer control is turned to low output. Because of the hum problem, it is not generally advisable to use tubular fluorescent lamps in bedrooms, although the hum may be imperceptible in other rooms because the ambient noise masks it.

How does two-position switching work?

Two-position switching (two-way switching) enables the control of a lighting point from two positions – for example, from the top and bottom of a staircase, or from two ends of a long corridor. The two switches used are not 'on-off' switches, but are 'change-over' switches which have an additional connection so that there are three wires linking them (see Figure 14.6).

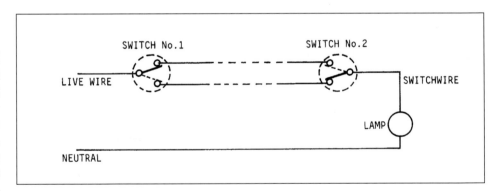

FIGURE 14.6
Two-position switching. The lamp can be switched on or off from either switch. Depending on the position of the toggle on the other switch, the position of the toggle of each switch may be either up or down.

What is delay switching?

After being switched on, delay switches automatically switch off after a set period. They are an energy-saving idea, allowing lights to be switched on when required without having to remember to switch them off. The normal condition for the lighting is 'off', and is selected to 'on' when someone wants to pass through the passage or use the stairs.

Delay switches may incorporate a mechanical delay (an air chamber or oil dashpot), but most modern delay switches incorporate a solid-state delay device. The delay is adjustable, usually between 30 seconds and 6 minutes. Delay switches may be used for on-off switching, or for two-position switching. Control may be by a toggle switch, a push button or a touch-plate control. A delay switch should have a glow lamp incorporated into it so that the user can find the switch in the dark.

Delay switches offer poor security, for unless the switch has been recently operated, the area will be in darkness, thus providing a hiding place for a mugger or wrongdoer. Therefore delay switching is not recommended for use in any place to which the public have access.

Delay switching was formerly much used for controlling lighting on staircases and common entrances in multiple-occupancy houses and blocks of flats to prevent waste and to save the cost and trouble of someone having to switch the lights on in the evening and switch them off late at night or next morning (if no time-switching device was used). Modern PE (photoelectric) switches and PIR proximity-detection switches have made delay switching obsolete. There is no longer an economic argument in favour of delay switching, for the operating cost per hour of modern sources (such as compact fluorescent lamps) is so low that all-night lighting – or even 24-hour lighting – is often justified.

What are touch-plate controllers?

The common arrangement is for the lights in a room to be switched from a position near the door. Under the cover of a conventional switchbox there is a metal or plastic box (a BESA box) which can house other types of control instead of the conventional on-off switch operated by a toggle or rocker.

Lighting controls that can be mounted within standard wall-mounted boxes include dimmers operated by a small rotatable knob, pressure-plate switches and touch-plate controllers.

A touch-plate controller is operated by simply placing one's hand upon it – no pressure is needed. Touching the plate will switch the light on; another touch will switch it off. The electronic circuit within the switch detects the presence of one's hand by the capacitance effect, and initiates the switching action.

A touch-plate controller can also be used to regulate a lighting dimmer (see Chapter 13). Placing one's hand on the switch-plate causes the circuit to 'cycle' through its range of dim to bright and back again, and one simply removes one's hand when the desired level of illuminance is reached.

What is the function of lighting track?

In its simplest form, lighting track consists merely of a linear support for a small number of directable spotlamps which are permanently connected to the supply by helical-coiled flexible cables. This popular type of fitting can be readily installed by DIY, and it does provide the means of positioning the spotlamps where desired along the track, and aiming them to produce a desired lighting effect. Strictly speaking, such fittings are not lighting track, but merely a form of 'cluster light', for the lighting fittings are permanently connected to the supply and not plugged into electrical conductors concealed in the track.

There is a wide variety of lighting track systems, ranging from simple single-circuit track into which mains-voltage spotlamps or downlighters, etc., can be plugged at any point, up to sophisticated tracks with four independent lighting circuits which may be at mains voltage or at low voltage (for low-voltage tungsten-halogen lamps). The track may incorporate the step-down transformer for these.

If a track with two or four separate circuits is to be installed, it must be connected to the mains supply at the ceiling rose, and each circuit must be wired to a switch or dimmer. The wiring for such a lighting track will be beyond the scope of ordinary DIY, and the services of a properly qualified electrician should be sought.

However, an even more sophisticated form of lighting track called *remotely controlled track* is just coming onto the market. This does not present the installation problems associated with conventional two-circuit and four-circuit track systems in which each circuit must be wired to an external switch or dimmer control. A remotely controlled track requires only a single connection to the existing ceiling rose. Its four or six circuits can be switched on or off, or dimmed, simply by pointing a coded infra-red controller at it – in exactly the same way that we control a television set.

How might the lighting of an indoor Christmas tree be made more attractive?

Christmas-tree lighting sets (which should only be purchased and used if they bear the BSI Kitemark or have BEAB approval to BS 4647) make a much more interesting spectacle if two chains of lights are used, the supplies to them being taken through a two-way flasher (or two separate flashers) so that the lights come on and off randomly every few seconds, giving the illusion of movement.

Some important safety matters: Flasher units should be of a pattern that has a screw-fixed insulating cover over the terminals so that children cannot tamper with them. Connections to the Christmas-tree lighting should be safely made through leads connected to fused plug-tops. If the leads are not long enough, *do not make a taped joint,* but use a line connector, or an extension lead fitted with a socket outlet as described earlier. Use the correct size of fuse in the plug-top (see Chapter 9). To guard against risk of fire or elec-

Connections to Christmas tree lights should be made through a plug-top containing a 3 Amp fuse and preferably using an RCD adaptor (see page 74) for greater safety.

tric shock, preferably the lead or leads from the tree lights will not be connected directly to a socket outlet, but will be plugged into an RCD adaptor inserted in the socket outlet (see Chapter 9).

The lit tree will be more attractive if the room lighting is subdued, so this is a situation where a dimmer for the room's general lighting would be valuable. For a children's party, changing some of the lamps in the room for coloured ones for the occasion will add to the festive appearance.

How may cornice lighting be installed?

If the ceiling height in a room is at least 2.5 m, it may be possible to use cornice lighting. This is a means of providing soft, well-diffused light across a room, without any light source being visible. It is an excellent way of deploying tubular fluorescent lamps to produce a comfortable – even luxurious – atmosphere in rooms of reasonable ceiling height. Before attempting either to install lighting in an existing cornice, or to install a new cornice or cove for the purpose of concealing lighting within it, it is advisable to draw a cross-section of the room to scale, and study the possible cut-off angle (see Figure 14.7).

Some existing plaster cornices will be found to be hollow. If the recess is deep, one may use batten fittings containing tubular fluorescent lamps. If it is shallow, the fluorescent tubular lamps may be mounted in 'Terry clips' and the control gear mounted separately. If the depth of the cornice is limited, the height of the front upstand might be raised by fitting a wooden or plaster beading so that the lamps are concealed. The objective is to ensure that the lamps cannot be seen by a taller-than-average person standing at the distant wall, i.e. the cut-off should be no lower than 2 m above the floor at the far wall.

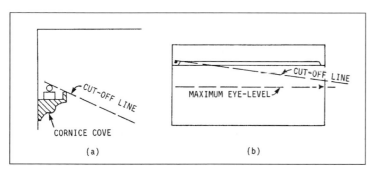

FIGURE 14.7
Cornice lighting. (a) In a case like this, the cut-off angle is too low for a wide room, and would have to be improved by fitting an upstand at the edge of the cornice, or by lowering the lamps within the cornice. (b) The objective is to conceal the lamps from being seen by a taller-than-average person standing at the far side of the room, i.e. to achieve a cut-off to about 2 m above the floor at the opposite wall.

To get a reasonably even spread of light across the ceiling, the cornice should be mounted not less than one-sixth of the room width down the ceiling. To get a good spread of light up the wall above the cornice, the lamps should be positioned as far off the wall as can be conveniently managed. The inside of the cornice (i.e. its upper face) should be painted matt white, and should be dusted as frequently as can be arranged to maintain its reflectance, and the tubes should also be kept clean.

To achieve the highest possible uniformity, only one length, power and phosphor colour of tubular fluorescent lamps should be used along a length of cornice. To make the brightness of the upper walls and ceiling reasonably uniform, there should be the minimum possible gap between the ends of the tubes, or – if the cove is wide enough – the tubes may be angled slightly and overlapped a few centimetres.

If separate control gear is employed, the components should be positioned so as not to throw shadows. If not screwed down firmly, they may emit hum.

If the idea of cornice lighting is appealing, but the technicalities and expense are daunting, consider using a limited length of cornice – on one wall, say. It can be quite effective to mount cornice lighting just over the windows, or, by allowing some downward light, to create a 'lighting pelmet'.

How is a lighting pelmet constructed?

A lighting pelmet is not an efficient means of getting light into a room, but it is highly decorative. A pelmet constructed of plywood or hardboard on a wooden frame can be used to conceal a curtain rail (see Figure 14.8). The pelmet is supported by end-pieces (and, in the case of very wide windows, by one or more intermediate brackets), so that there is space to mount one or more tubular fluorescent lamps. These will distribute light upward (if the pelmet has an open top) and also downward on the curtains in an attractive manner. If the lamps are close to the curtains, the lighting effect will be confined to a narrow band at the head of the curtains, and this will not be so effective. Mounting the lamps close to the curtains also creates a degree of fire risk.

The inside of the pelmet should be painted matt white. The general effect will be better if the wall above the window is of a light colour. By placing the lamps high in the pelmet, a better spread of light across the ceiling will be obtained. The outside of the pelmet may be painted, or covered with the same material as that of the curtaining.

The lamps used could be linear architectural lamps, but then the running cost and cost of replacement lamps would be high, so fluorescent tubular lamps are generally preferred. If a standard length of fluorescent tubular lamp conveniently spans the pelmet, the installation will be simpler; if two or more shorter lamps must be used to make up the length, they should be butted end-to-end as closely as possible. In order to bring the lamps forward, better results are generally obtained by mounting the lamps in Terry clips on the inner face of the vertical pelmet board and using separate control gear.

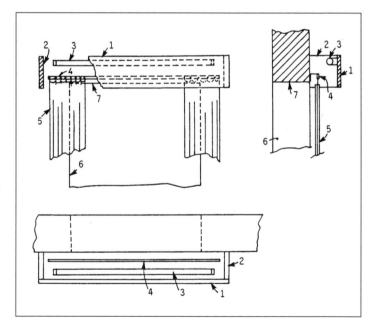

FIGURE 14.8
Construction of an open-topped lighting pelmet. (1) Pelmet. (2) End-cheeks. (3) Lamp or lamps. (4) Curtain rail. (5) Curtain. (6) Cheek of window. (7) Soffit of window.

It is only feasible to install lighting into an existing pelmet box with a closed top if the box is of generous dimensions to permit ventilation to keep the lamp(s) cool. Of course, a closed-top pelmet will not allow any light to flow upward. Generally, it would be better to modify a closed-top pelmet to open-top construction to allow ventilation and an upward flow of light.

The power supply to the lamps in a pelmet can be carried up inconspicuously from the skirting board in a vertical run of mini-trunking positioned close to the window frame. If necessary, the mini-trunking can be painted the same colour as the window frame.

How might one light a dark cupboard?

A deep cupboard or larder will be more usable if it is fitted with a light. A utilitarian method would be to fit a 'batten lampholder' to take a 25 W or 40 W filament lamp. If the lamp can be positioned above the cupboard door, it will not cause glare and will be less vulnerable to damage. A tubular fluorescent lamp or a compact fluorescent lamp would neither be economical nor suitable in this location; a linear architectural lamp might be more appropriate, preferably contained in a small enclosed diffusing fitting, similar to a bathroom mirror light (often termed a 'striplight').

The light could be controlled by a switch positioned within the cupboard or outside it, but this means that the lamp might be left on inadvertently – which would be a waste of energy, and there could be a risk of the cupboard overheating. A better plan is to install a *door switch* which switches on the light when the door is opened and switches it off when the door is closed. Any door switch used should be fully insulated, i.e. its terminals protected by an insulating cover.

FIGURE 14.9
Door switch for a cupboard light. When the door is closed, the plunger must be depressed only the correct distance to open the switch.

FIGURE 14.10
Combined door switch and lamp for cupboard lighting. This incorporates a small lamp (usually a 15 W pigmy sign lamp) and proper means of gripping the cable. In this type, the plunger can be fully depressed without damaging the switch.

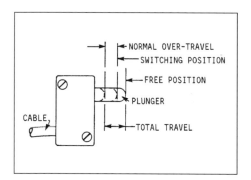

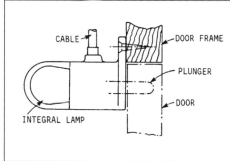

The common type of door switch (see Figure 14.9) has a spring-loaded plunger, and must be adjusted to ensure that the plunger is depressed the correct distance when the door is closed. Another type of door switch (see Figure 14.10) incorporates a lamp and is simpler to install.

What precautions should be taken when fitting cupboard lights?

The lamp should be positioned so that it will not be readily damaged, and so that it will not come into contact with the contents of the cupboard – for example, coats hanging on a rail. The heat from even a small lamp, left on for a long period in an unventilated cupboard, could cause fire.

Before replacing a failed or broken lamp that is controlled by a door switch, remember that opening the door will make the circuit live, therefore the circuit should be isolated for safety. Some patterns of combined miniature lighting fitting and door switch (see Figure 14.10) can be isolated by unplugging the connector when relamping.

How could a wall recess or alcove be used to house a lighted display, say, of glassware or pottery?

Many rooms have a recess or alcove on each side of the chimney breast. These recesses could be attractively converted by building a pelmet light at the top, either at ceiling level or lower down according to the height of the room and the nature of the planned display. The treatment can be varied to suit personal taste and the general style of the decor of the room. The pelmet may contain a tubular fluorescent lamp, and possibly it could conceal some miniature fittings housing low-voltage tungsten-halogen dichroic spotlamps, so that objects displayed – say, on glass shelves within the recess – are attractively lit. Additional lighting at the edges of shelves or concealed under them could also be applied (see Figure 14.11).

How may wall-mounted lighting fittings be installed?

As pointed out in Chapter 2, the time for fitting wall-mounted lights is undoubtedly when the walls are stripped for redecorating. If the wiring to wall-mounted lighting fittings is installed by a properly qualified electrician, it will probably be connected into a permanently wired lighting circuit in the ceiling cavity or attic above. The wires will be brought through the ceiling in a vertical run to the lighting point, concealed in a channel chased into the wall, and then plastered over. A switchbox could be recessed into the wall below the wall-mounted fitting for a switch to control it.

Note: When fixing anything to a wall by means of masonry nails or screws, always assume that there may be cables concealed in the wall vertically above or below any wall-mounted light or switch, etc.

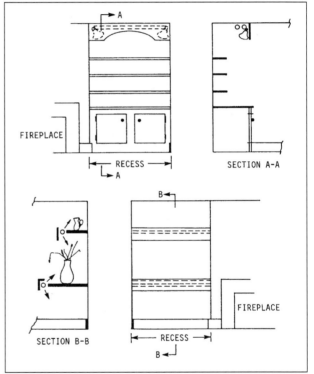

FIGURE 14.11
Brightening a room recess. Section A-A shows a pelmet behind which can be mounted a tubular fluorescent lamp and/or some iniature spotlamps to light the glass shelves and cupboard top. Section B-B shows how tubular fluorescent lamps may be mounted on the front edge of shelves to create a striking display. Such 'display lighting' contributes to the general brightness of the whole room.

You may desire to install a wall-mounted fitting without chasing the wall, perhaps with a view to recessing the wiring at some future time. At DIY level, the supply could be carried up to the lighting fitting by a vertical run of surface-mounted mini-trunking, the connection being made by a fused plug to a permanently installed socket outlet at skirting-board level generally, as shown in Figure 14.5.

The use of plug-in wall-bracket connectors is recommended, for these enable the wiring to be installed but for the actual installation of the lighting fitting to be delayed until the room decorations are complete. Also, on future occasions (for example, when the room is being redecorated) the wall-mounted lighting fittings can be easily removed and restored without disturbing the wiring.

How can one install some emergency lighting in the home?

The subject of emergency lighting is introduced in Chapter 2. Emergency lighting fittings provide light to enable persons to escape from premises during a fire or other emergency when the normal lighting has failed. They switch themselves on automatically when the mains supply fails, and remain functioning long enough to enable people to get out of the building. When the supply is restored after a mains interruption, the batteries within the units automatically recommence recharging.

The simplest form of emergency lighting, and that which is usually appropriate in dwellings is a 'single-point emergency luminaire'. This contains a small fluorescent lamp, with its own rechargeable battery and control gear. Single-point emergency lighting luminaires come in two types, either as exit signs or as enclosed lighting fittings suitable for wall or ceiling mounting. The latter come in quite attractive designs, which can be used for lighting passageways and stairs in place of other lighting fittings.

If a single-point emergency lighting fitting is installed in place of existing fitting and connected to the house wiring, it can operate continuously, or be controlled by a PE controller, or be switched on and off like an ordinary light (and will come on automatically on mains failure whatever the position of the control switch).

Modern emergency lighting fittings to BS 5266 contain sealed batteries which require no topping up. The manufacturer's instructions regarding the method of installation should be followed, particularly noting that some emergency lighting units are suitable for mounting only in certain attitudes, e.g. which way up on a wall, or if suitable for ceiling mounting, etc. Read and follow carefully any maintenance or periodic testing instructions provided with the emergency lighting fitting.

More information about emergency lighting and escape from fires in dwellings is given in a book *Emergency Lighting for Industrial, Commercial and Residential Premises* (see References).

Installing
EXTERIOR LIGHTING

How should exterior-type lighting fittings be stored before use?

Some general guidelines regarding receiving and unpacking new lighting fittings are given in Chapter 14. Lighting fittings designed for outdoor installation are protected against humidity and the entry of moisture in normal use. But, before installation, they can be attacked by corrosion internally if the conduit entry is not blocked off to prevent the penetration of moisture and damp. The fittings should be stored in a dry, normally heated room until you desire to install them.

What special requirements apply to outdoor electrical installations?

Moisture is a conductor of electricity. Because exterior lighting fittings and installations are used in the presence of moisture in the form of snow, rain or condensation, they must be installed with special care to ensure safety. All outdoor wiring must be contained within impervious enclosures, and all metalwork must be earthed.

There should be no problems in connecting lighting by means of fused plugs into properly installed external waterproof socket outlets. The supply to such a socket outlet should be protected by an RCD (see Chapter 9), and the installation of external socket outlets and the cabling thereto should be carried out by a properly qualified electrician who will ensure that buried cables are protected from accidental damage by sharp spades or a post being driven into the ground at some time in the future. Surface runs of cables in conduit, say, along a fence or on the exterior of a building, must be robustly installed in watertight conduit – again, a job for a properly qualified electrician.

If outdoor waterproof socket outlets are installed for use with garden lighting and lawnmowers, etc., or if watertight switches are located in the garden to control floodlighting, etc., it is recommended that they should be located under a canopy or otherwise sheltered from rain.

Leads, in the form of heavy-duty flexible cable, may be connected to a socket outlet in the house to supply temporarily installed spike lamps, etc., and such circuits must be protected by a *residual current device* (RCD) as explained in Chapter 9. Great care should be taken to prevent damage to the flexible cables, including ensuring that they do not get trapped in a window or door closure.

How might one light a front porch?

The positioning of a lighting fitting in a porch will depend on the physical layout of the porch. A suitable type of fitting for a typical porch would be a bulkhead fitting or a decorative lantern which may be mounted on the ceiling of the porch, on the wall above the door or on one of the side walls. Choose a mounting position that will ensure that the approach to the door and any steps leading up to it are well illuminated, and that a person calling at the front door will be clearly revealed. By considering how a lighting fitting will spread its light and cast shadows if mounted in various alternative positions, the best mounting position can be selected.

If the light is to be switched on and off frequently, a filament lamp should be used. But if the light is to be left on all evening regularly, or if it forms part of all-night lighting used for security, then a compact fluorescent lamp will be the most suitable and economical.

For a typical porch at a house in a street that has streetlighting, the lighting fitting should house a lamp of about 800 lumens output (say, a 60 W filament lamp or a 14 W 2D compact fluorescent lamp). If a large area of steps is to be lit, or if it is desired to cast light along the front path, use a lamp giving around 1,200 lumens output (say, a 100 W filament lamp or a 25 W SL lamp).

How may exterior lighting fittings be controlled?

Manual switching and PIR control are suitable to control filament lamps, but are not recommended for control of compact fluorescent lamps which take up to a minute to come to full brightness, and rather longer in cold weather. Where use of a lamp is intermittent, there would be only limited economic benefit from using a CFL, as the total hours of use per annum are few, and so the best choice would be a filament lamp.

PIR switching is a useful method of control for lighting at the rear of the house, where no security function is intended.

For security lighting applications and for other dusk-to-dawn lighting where you do not want the chore of switching the lights on every evening and off every morning, photoelectric control (PE control) is the best choice.

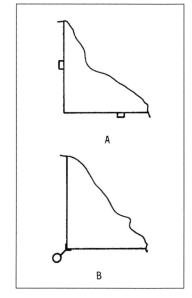

FIGURE 15.1
View A shows the use of two wall-mounted bulkhead fittings. View B shows how a similar distribution of light along the faces of the two walls could be obtained by the use of one 'jam-jar' lighting fitting mounted on a corner-mounting bracket.

How could one provide a simple system of security lighting for a typical home?

The benefits and the economics of domestic security lighting are discussed in Chapter 8. The best choice of lamps for this application are energy-efficient compact fluorescent lamps.

Security lighting systems should be in operation from dusk to dawn, every night, and are best controlled by a photoelectric switch (PE switch). The PE switch will switch the lights on at dusk even when there is no one at home. Compact fluorescent lamps of types with claimed lives of up to 8,000 hours or more will require replacement only at intervals of about two years. Between relampings, the only attention needed may be to give the lighting fitting enclosures a wipe over with a damp cloth from time to time.

If the district brightness is low, only a little light is needed to deter most wrongdoers from attacking your premises after dark. For a typical semi-detached suburban house, you would require two – or possibly three – lighting fittings. One fitting should be positioned near the front door, and one or two at the rear and side of the house to protect the rear entrance and ground-floor windows (and also to make it safer to go outside after dark). You may also need one to provide light along a side access way or drive.

A single lighting fitting in exactly the right place might do the job that would otherwise require the use of two or more fittings. For example, it may be possible to position one lighting fitting on a corner bracket so that it sheds light in two directions, thereby reducing the number of lighting fittings required (see Figure 15.1).

For a typical semi-detached house, two or three carefully sited lighting fittings will leave no dark corner where an intruder might hide (see Figure 15.2). Note that if a lighting fitting is positioned over the garage doors (as suggested in Chapter 7), it could be switched with the other lighting fittings and form part of your security lighting installation.

The PE controller can be a separate device which is used to control a group of lighting fittings, or it may be integral with the lighting fitting. Note that if there are two or more fittings to be controlled, the PE controller in one of them can switch the others too.

Your choice of compact fluorescent lamp will depend upon whether you purchase lighting fittings that come complete with integral control gear for a particular type of CFL lamp, or if you buy simple fittings such as 'jam-jar'

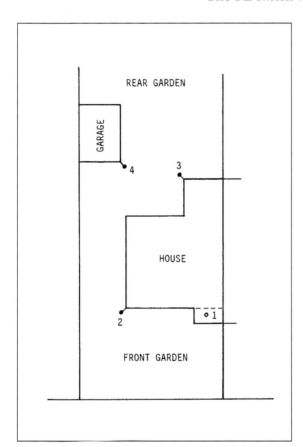

FIGURE 15.2
Security lighting for a typical semi-detached house. (1) A lighting fitting located in the porch. (2) and (3) 'Jam-jar' lighting fittings mounted on the corners of the building. If fitting (4) was mounted on the garage as shown, it would be possible to dispense with fitting (3).

119

fittings which can be used with filament lamps or with compact fluorescent lamps (see Figure 15.3). In the latter case you will use a 'retrofit' type of compact fluorescent lamp, e.g. a lamp with integral control gear, such as Types SL, SLD and 2D.

As regards lamp wattages, remember that the lower the district brightness, the less light you will need to get a sufficient degree of brightness and therefore a good deterrent effect. In very dark conditions, lamps giving around 200 to 400 lumens will be adequate in the lighting systems described. If the district brightness is high, or if the areas to be lit are larger, you will need lamps giving around 400 to 800 lumens. The types of compact fluorescent lamps and their comparative lumen outputs are listed in Figure 11.5.

What safety precautions are necessary with regard to the use of garden spike lamps?

The use of garden spike lamps is described in Chapter 8. It is strongly advised that only the size and power of PAR lamp recommended by the garden-spike maker be used (usually a PAR-38 80 W clear or coloured lamp). Correctly fitted, a flexible gland makes a watertight seal with the envelope of the lamp, so that the fitting is safe to use, and the lamp is not likely to shatter if rained on or sprinkled with the garden hose. If the wrong type or size of lamp were to be used, the unit would not be sealed, and there could be danger of electric shock.

A spike lamp is normally supplied complete with a length of special tough, flexible cable connected to the fitting with a watertight seal. Do not tamper with this seal. If the cable supplied is not long enough, it can be extended by the use of a watertight in-line cable connector. The flexible cable should be plugged into a socket outlet protected with a residual current device (see Chapter 9). Spike lamps should be regarded as a temporary lighting feature, not for permanent installation. The plug should be removed from its socket and the unit taken into the house when it is not being used. *Caution:* Do not attempt to remove or replace the lamp in the lampholder of a spike lamp while the lead is plugged in.

What safety precautions are necessary regarding the use of festoon lighting?

Festoon lighting is introduced in Chapter 8. If one follows the maker's instructions, festoon lighting presents no special risks; but the following cautions should be observed.

Lampholders on festoon lighting should be *moulded on to the cable*, and not be of a type that has sharp contacts that bite through the insulation of the cable to make connection with the cores – such are potential killers.

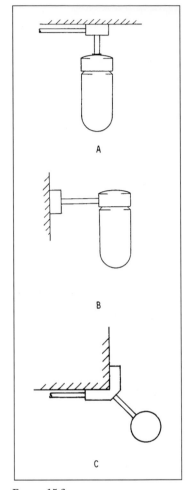

FIGURE 15.3
Mounting of 'jam-jar' (wellglass) lighting fittings. A: Top mounting. B: Side mounting. C: Corner-bracket mounting.

Spike lamps, fitted with coloured PAR bulbs, lie unnoticed in the garden during the day; but when switched on at dusk they can give the whole garden a fairyland look.

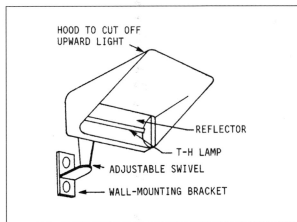

FIGURE 15.4
Typical small 'shovel' floodlight for linear tungsten-halogen lamp. Suitable for floodlighting a domestic garden.

Do not attempt to join lengths of festoon lighting except with proper exterior-pattern connectors which will be safe in the rain. Do not operate a festoon if it has a broken lamp, or if the enclosure to any lamp is missing or damaged. Do not attempt to remove or replace a lamp while the festoon is plugged in to the mains.

How may garden floodlights be installed?

In Chapter 8 it was mentioned that tungsten-halogen lamps are suitable for floodlighting a domestic garden. These small linear lamps are used in a type of floodlight (shaped rather like a small inverted shovel) that emits a wide flat-topped beam and gives no upward light (see Figure 15.4). The lamp is intensely bright, especially when seen at night. The floodlights should be mounted not less than 3 m above ground level, and preferably higher.

If the floodlight fittings are mounted on the back wall of the house a little higher than first-floor window-sill level and near the windows, you will be able to reach them from the windows without recourse to use of a ladder when adjusting them and later when relamping them.

For suburban gardens of typical size, a quite good effect can be produced by using one 200 W, 300 W or 500 W tungsten-halogen lamp. Two fittings produce a better effect if they can be spaced widely apart so that the shadows are softened.

After installation, careful adjustment of the floodlights is necessary on two grounds. First, it is essential that the tungsten-halogen lamp in a flood-light of this kind is mounted absolutely horizontally, for otherwise the halide gas in the linear lamp envelope will migrate to the lower end, and the life of the lamp will be short.

The second adjustment will be to direct the beams so that they cover your garden, and do not send too much light sideways into your neighbours' gardens. Having got the general directions right, you must then adjust the 'angle of tilt', to ensure that the top of the beam of the floodlight is aimed no higher than the top of your back fence. By careful aiming – keep most of the light within the area of your garden and ensure that you do not cause nuisance to either near or distant neighbours.

How can one provide lighting to enable a garden swimming pool to be used at night?

With the right equipment, properly installed, wonderful effects – including underwater lighting – can be used safely. The subject is dealt with in a book called *Design and Planning of Swimming Pools* which is listed in the References. The lighting of swimming pools is a specialised subject, and it is strongly recommended that such lighting should only be installed by properly qualified electricians who are experts in pool lighting.

In Chapter 2 we introduced the fascinating subject of fibre-optic light-guides, and in Chapter 8 we noted that these may provide an excellent and safe way of lighting domestic garden swimming pools. With the lamp that feeds the fibre-optics installed in the house, the light-conducting optical fibres can be led out into the garden in complete safety, for they carry no electricity and do not get hot. Again, it will pay you to get advice from experts, such as the company Absolute Action Ltd which offers a consultancy service regarding fibre-optic lighting.

At the lowest level of technical difficulty, one could provide lighting at the pool by simply directing floodlights on to it, the floodlights being mounted on the back wall of the house or other convenient structure, as described in the previous answer regarding garden floodlighting.

CHAPTER 16

Some SAFETY DO'S and DONT'S

- DON'T undertake any changes to the permanent wiring of your home unless you are skilled in electrical matters. If you need help, DO employ only a properly qualified electrician to undertake alterations, additions or connections to the fixed electrical installation in your home.

- DO have a residual current device (RCD) installed at your consumer unit to give protection against earth faults on your wiring installation. DO regularly operate the test button on this device to keep it in peak condition.

- DO consider changing an old-fashioned consumer unit with fuses for a modern one with miniature circuit-breakers (MCBs) to control and protect the circuits.

- DO ensure that every portable lighting fitting or electrical appliance fed from a socket outlet is protected by the correct size of fuse in the plug-top. See Chapter 9 for the simple method of determining the correct size of fuse for any load.

- DON'T risk overloading any circuit by trying to cram extra wires into connectors or three-pin plugs. Each three-pin plug should have only one lead attached to it unless it is a special type designed to connect several cables.

- DON'T try to plug a three-pin adaptor into another three-pin adaptor – it is likely to fall out or make a poor connection and overheat. Three-pin adaptors may be used, but if you have insufficient socket outlets, it is better to install more socket outlets or use a multi-socket adaptor as described in Chapters 9 and 14.

- DO use an RCD adaptor in socket outlets that feed portable lighting fittings – especially Christmas tree lights, and in any socket outlet in the house that supplies lighting used out of doors.

- DON'T make taped joints in cables. If a flexible lead is too short, either replace it with a longer one or extend it by use of a three-pin line connector or a multi-way adaptor (see Chapter 14).

- DON'T use a bayonet-cap adaptor (BC adaptor plug) to make a connection into a BC lampholder – *ever!* If you have any single-way or two-way BC lampholder adaptor plugs in the house at this moment, DO take them out to the dustbin now and dispose of them. They are potential killers.

- DON'T attempt to use any lighting fitting or electrical appliance outside the house unless it is connected by a three-core flexible lead fed from a circuit containing a residual current device (RCD) (see Chapters 9 and 15).

- DON'T take any portable lighting fitting or portable electrical appliance into the bathroom (see Chapter 5).

- DON'T put portable lighting fittings in the bedrooms of small children. A portable nightlight fitting should be placed so that it is well out of the reach of a small child in a cot (see Chapter 5).

- DON'T fix any lighting fitting to a combustible surface such as a hardboard partition.

- DO remember that the intense concentrated beam from any spotlight fitting (and especially from a low-voltage tungsten-halogen spotlamp) may be hot enough to ignite flammable materials such as curtains if they are too close to the lamp (see Chapters 11 and 12).

- DON'T allow curtains to come into contact with any kind of lighting fitting (see Chapter 12).

- DON'T attempt to recess into the ceiling any type of spotlight, downlighter, etc., which is designed for surface mounting, for this could result in it overheating and could cause a fire.

- DON'T buy a free-standing uplighter unless it is fitted with a tilt switch (see Chapter 12).

- DON'T put a larger wattage of filament lamp into a lighting fitting than the fitting was designed for. If the lighting fitting you buy is not already marked with the correct size and type of lamp, DO mark the fitting indelibly with this information before putting it into use.

- DON'T discard any manufacturers' instruction leaflets which come with your new lighting fittings, but keep them safely for the time when you may need to refer to them.

Useful names and addresses

CHARTERED INSTITUTION OF BUILDING SERVICES ENGINEERS
Delta House, 222 Balham High Road,
London SW12 9BS
Tel: 0181-675 5211 Fax: 0181-675 5449
- The Lighting Division of CIBSE is a professional body for lighting engineers. Its publications recommend good practice relating to many aspects of lighting; publishers of the *Code for Interior Lighting.*

ELECTRICAL CONTRACTORS ASSOCIATION (ECA)
ESCA House, 34 Palace Court, London W2 4HY
Tel: 0171-229 1266 Fax: 0171-221 7344
- A trade association of electrical installation contractors. Members of the ECA employ properly qualified electricians.

ELECTRICITY ASSOCIATION
30 Millbank, London SW1P 4RD
Tel: 0171-834 2333 Fax: 0171-931 0356
- An organisation of the electricity supply industry concerned with the marketing of electrical energy by the electricity supply companies in the UK.

INSTITUTION OF LIGHTING ENGINEERS, THE
Lennox House, 9 Lawford Road, Rugby CV21 2DZ
Tel: (01788) 576492 Fax: (01788) 540145
- A professional institution concerned with all aspects of lighting.

LIGHTING ASSOCIATION, THE
Stafford Park 7, Telford, Shropshire TF3 3BD
Tel: (01952) 290905 Fax: (01952) 290906
- A trade association of lighting manufacturers, distributors and retailers, concerned with the provision of safe and good quality domestic lighting.

LIGHTING INDUSTRY FEDERATION, THE
Swan House, 207 Balham High Road,
London SW17 7BQ
Tel: 0181-675 5432 Fax: (0181) 673 5880
- A trade association of lampmakers and manufacturers of lighting fittings which has done much to promote high standards of safety and quality in lighting products.

NATIONAL INSPECTION COUNCIL FOR ELECTRICAL INSTALLATION CONTRACTING, THE
Vintage House, 37 Albert Embankment,
London SE1 7UJ
Tel: 0171-582 7746; Fax: 0171-820 0831
- A consumer safety body dedicated to the safety of users of electricity. There are 10,500 electrical contractors enrolled with NICEIC.

PARTIALLY SIGHTED SOCIETY
Queen's Road, Doncaster, South Yorkshire DN1 2NX
Tel: (01302) 368998
- A charity that provides helpful advice for the visually handicapped.

ROYAL SOCIETY FOR THE PREVENTION OF ACCIDENTS
Cannon House, The Priory, Queensway,
Birmingham B4 6BS
Tel: (0121) 200 2461
- The leading national authority on all aspects of safety and accident prevention in the UK.

Note: The telephone numbers shown have been amended by the addition of a number 1 inserted after the initial 0 in the area codes. These changes will run in parallel with the old numbers after August 1994, and will come into effect from 16 April 1995. If you have any difficulties in calling any of these numbers, expert help is available on (0800) 01 01 01.

References

BS 7671: IEE WIRING REGULATIONS, 16th edn, The British Standards Institution and the Institution of Electrical Engineers. These Regulations are the basis for all the safety instructions given in this book. It is unlikely that the home DIYer would ever need to refer to them, but, when employing an electrical contractor, it should be a contract condition that all work shall be carried out in compliance with these Regulations.

CODE FOR INTERIOR LIGHTING, 1994, Chartered Institution of Building Services Engineers (Lighting Division). Gives recommendations on lighting practice for a wide variety of interiors and tasks, although it does not provide recommendations specifically for domestic lighting.

DESIGN AND PLANNING OF SWIMMING POOLS Dawes, John, 2nd edn, John Dawes Publications, 1986. This book has been adopted as a handbook by the Institute of Swimming Pool Engineers (ISPE). It contains guidance on electrical installations for swimming pools, including underwater lighting. Its electrical safety practices are aligned with the objectives of the *IEE WIRING REGULATIONS*.

ENERGY EFFICIENCY IN DOMESTIC APPLIANCES, HMSO, 1990.

EMERGENCY LIGHTING FOR INDUSTRIAL, COMMERCIAL AND RESIDENTIAL PREMISES, Lyons, Stanley, Butterworth-Heinemann, 1992. This includes explanations of emergency lighting principles, guidelines on selecting equipment, a buyer's guide and an appendix on fires in dwellings.

Glossary and Index

Here are simple definitions of some common lighting terms and references to important topics dealt with in this book.

ARCHITECTURAL LAMP (also called an architectural tubular lamp)
A tungsten-filament lamp with a linear filament contained in a tubular envelope which may be of clear or opal-diffusing glass. Single-ended and double-ended lamps of this type are available. They are used in mirror lights and picture lights. Curved and circular versions of these lamps are available. See page 83.

BALLAST
See *Control gear.*

BOLLARD, ILLUMINATED
A short column, the base of which is planted in the ground, that embodies a lamp. The light is mainly directed downward to help to demarcate a drive, etc., and give guidance to pedestrians at night. See page 59.

BULB
Popular term for a filament lamp.

BULKHEAD FITTING
A compact, fully enclosed lighting fitting designed for outdoor use, typically for attachment to a vertical surface or for use under a canopy.

BUTTERFLY BOLTS
See *Toggle Bolts.*

CANDLE LAMPS
Low-wattage filament lamps in clear or diffusing envelopes for use in candelabra fittings. See Figure 11.3.

CASING AND CAPPING
See *Mini-trunking.*

CEILING ROSE
Electric point for a ceiling-mounted lighting fitting. One type permits instant removal or replacement of a lighting fitting without disturbing the wiring. See page 16.

CEILING TRACK
See *Track.*

CFL
A compact fluorescent lamp.

CHANDELIER
Originally a device for holding wax candles, and generally applied to pendant lighting fittings, especially those that mimic a wax-candle chandelier, e.g. by the use of 'candle lamps'.

CHOKE
A term formerly used to denote an inductive *Ballast.*

COMPACT FLUORESCENT LAMP (also called CFL)
A low-power fluorescent tubular lamp in which the tube or tubes are bent to form a compact mass. Some types of CFL are suitable for 'retrofit', i.e. you simply insert the lamp into the BC or ES lampholder of an existing lighting fitting to replace the filament lamp. All types of CFL have to be operated with control gear which, according to type, may be 'integral' (i.e. it forms part of the lamp assembly and must be discarded along with the lamp at the end of lamp life), or 'reusable' (you only have to replace the 'lamp' part at the end of lamp life). See Chapter 11.

CONTROL GEAR (also called Ballast)
A device to regulate and control the current through a fluorescent tubular lamp. Control gear may be 'inductive' (i.e. consisting of a wire coil wound on a laminated iron core), or 'solid state' (i.e. electronic).

Inductive control gear is generally heavier and bulkier than solid-state control gear, and – at present – sometimes cheaper. Solid-state ballasts are lighter, smaller, quieter, and have smaller energy losses than that of inductive control gear. Lamps with solid-state control gear operating at high frequency exhibit no flicker.

CONTROLLERS
See *Touch-plate controllers.*

CORNER BRACKET
A support for a small lighting fitting, typically for a 'jam-jar' (wellglass) pendant fitting, so that it may be mounted on an external corner and shed light along two walls that are at right-angles.

CORNICE LIGHTING
Lighting system in which the lamps are concealed by being placed in an architectural cornice and direct their light to the ceiling and upper walls. See *Cove lights.*

COVE LIGHTS
An architectural lighting fitment, similar to a cornice, containing lamps, applied to the upper walls of a room, the light from which is directed to the ceiling and upper walls. The lamps (typically tubular fluorescent lamps) are completely concealed from normal angles of view.

CROWN-SILVERED LAMPS
A type of filament lamp, used with a parabolic reflector, which produces an intensely bright, narrow beam. Popular for lighting small objects such as dartboards, but now being replaced by low-voltage tungsten-halogen lamps which are much more compact.

DAYLIGHT SWITCH
See *Photoelectric switch.*

DELAY SWITCHING
See Chapter 14.

DICHROIC REFLECTORS
Very efficient reflectors which are made by the 'dichroic' or 'thin-film' technology. The miniature reflectors used in low-voltage tungsten-halogen (LVTH) lamps are of this type.

DIFFUSER
Means of reducing the brightness of a source without significantly reducing the total amount of light emitted, as in the use of 'pearl' and 'opal' diffusing glass bulbs on filament lamps. The enclosures to some lighting fittings are made of diffusing glass or plastic material which conceals the lamp but transmits its light, the enclosure itself being luminous but not as bright as the bare lamp would be. See *Flashing.*

DISCHARGE LAMP
Any kind of lamp in which light is generated by the passage of a diffuse electric arc through a gas, including all fluorescent lamps. High-intensity discharge lamps (HID lamps) such as metal halide lamps are not commonly used for domestic lighting at present.

ELECTRONIC CONTROL GEAR
See *Ballast.*

ELECTRONIC PAR LAMP
A miniature LVTH lamp or HID lamp which is housed in the same type of envelope as a PAR lamp, complete with its electronic control gear. The HID version is not considered suitable for domestic use.

EMERGENCY LIGHTING
Lighting that is powered by a rechargeable battery, and is designed to come into operation automatically upon failure of the normal electrical supply. When the supply is available, the battery is automatically kept in a good state of charge. Emergency lighting fittings may be 'maintained' (i.e. they are constantly illuminated, operating from the normal supply when it is available, and operating from the battery when the normal supply fails), or 'non-maintained' (i.e. they switch on automatically when the normal supply fails). They may also be manually switched, and will operate from the normal supply when it is available, and be powered by the battery supply when the normal supply fails.

EYEBALL FITTINGS
Type of adjustable spotlamp fitting in which the lamp and its reflector are contained within a housing and can be directed at the required angle. May be surface mounted or ceiling recessed. See page 24.

FIBRE-OPTIC LIGHT CONDUCTORS
These are described in Chapter 2. Their use for applications such as garden pool lighting is discussed in Chapters 8 and 15.

FILAMENT LAMP
The term used in this book to designate the common form of incandescent lamps used in our homes (which are also called tungsten-filament lamps, tungsten lamps, GLS lamps, 'bulbs' or 'lightbulbs'). A lamp in which light is emitted from a white-hot filament of tungsten which is enclosed within a glass bulb. See Chapter 11.

FLASHER
A device that interrupts a circuit rhythmically, for example, to flash the lights on a festoon or on a Christmas tree.

FLASHING
The spread of light over a diffuser. A good diffuser is uniformly bright, i.e. it is well-flashed.

FLOODLIGHT
A lighting fitting employing a linear source (such as a tungsten-halogen lamp), in which the reflector is designed to emit a broad, flat-topped beam with little or no upward light. Exterior floodlights are commonly used for illuminating horizontal areas, gardens etc., and there are wall-washer fittings which employ the same principle.

FLOOR STANDARD
A tall, free-standing lighting fitting with a heavy base, usually fitted with a translucent shade, which distributes its light upward and downward, and also sideways in a diffuse manner. Also called a standard lamp.

FLUORESCENT LAMP
A lamp in which light is generated by the passage of a diffuse electric discharge through a low-pressure mercury-vapour filling, the resultant ultraviolet radiation being converted into visible light by the coating of phosphor powder which lines the inner surface of the enclosing glass tube. Tubular fluorescent lamps and compact fluorescent lamps (CFLs) work on this principle. See Chapter 11.

GENERAL LIGHTING
Lighting in an internal area which is provided for safety of movement and good appearance. The general lighting may be capable of being dimmed. In most rooms there will also be a requirement for 'local lighting', e.g. portable lighting fittings such as table lamps, desk lamps, etc.

GLS LAMP
Term used in the electrical trade for a filament lamp, the letters GLS standing for 'general lighting service'.

HALOGEN LAMP
A confusing term, for it can refer either to a tungsten-halogen lamp or a metal-halide lamp (which is a type of HID lamp not usually employed in home lighting).

HID LAMP
A high-intensity discharge lamp. Such lamps are generally unsuitable for domestic lighting purposes.

INDUCTIVE (as in 'inductive ballast')
See *Ballast*.

JAM-JAR FITTING
Informal name for a type of enclosed exterior luminaire (properly called a 'wellglass fitting') with a glass or plastic enclosure like a jar and a top canopy which may be designed for suspension, top mounting to a canopy, or wall mounting. Top- and side-mounting versions can fit to a wall bracket, swan-neck bracket or corner bracket. Extensively used with a filament lamp or compact fluorescent lamp. Some models incorporate a PIR or PE device.

LAMP
Use of this word can be confusing, for it has two meanings; it can mean any kind of lightsource, and it

can also mean a lighting fitting such as a table lamp.

LAMPADIER
A term sometimes used in the USA to denote what would be called a table lamp in the UK.

LIGHTING FITTING (sometimes called a light fitting)
A luminaire, i.e. any device that contains a lamp of any kind.

LIGHTING TRACK
See *TRACK*.

LIGHTSOURCE
A device that converts electrical energy into light (commonly called a lamp). Lightsources used in the home include filament lamps, compact fluorescent lamps, fluorescent tubular lamps, and tungsten-halogen lamps.

LINE CONNECTOR
A plug-and-socket device for connecting two flexible cables together to gain a greater length. See Chapter 14.

LOCAL LIGHTING
Lighting that is provided to augment the general lighting of a room, to provide additional illumination for tasks, dining, etc., or to produce a pleasant lighting effect.

LOSSES
Energy consumed unproductively by a lamp or its ballast. Lost energy is converted to heat.

LOW-VOLTAGE TUNGSTEN-HALOGEN LAMPS
Miniature prefocused spotlamp lamps which operate on a low-voltage supply obtained from a step-down transformer. Because of their compact size they are suitable for use in clusters on lighting track. LVTH lamps are also used in some portable lighting fittings, especially desk lamps, in which a step-down transformer is incorporated. See page 92.

LUMINAIRE
Proper name for a lighting fitting, i.e. any device that contains a lamp of any kind.

LVTH
See *Low-voltage tungsten-halogen lamps*.

MINI-TRUNKING
A type of miniature trunking for concealing and protecting surface-run wiring, consisting of a shallow plastic channel and a cover strip which snaps on to it, as well as corner pieces, T-junctions and boxes for housing switches, socket outlets, etc. A range of sizes is available. Popular sizes for domestic DIY installations are 16 mm x 16 mm and 25 mm x 13 mm. See Chapter 14.

MIRROR LIGHT
Any type of lighting fitting designed for mounting above, below or either side of a mirror to aid the subject to see her or his face for make-up or shaving, etc.

MUSHROOM LAMP
Popular term for a blown-glass reflector lamp.

NEON (or Neon tube)
Terms that are sometimes quite wrongly applied to tubular fluorescent lamps. (Actually, neon is a rare gas which is used in some lamps. A neon tube is a type of luminous tube which emits red light, and is used in advertising signs.)

NOISE FROM LIGHTING FITTINGS
See Chapter 14.

'NON-SLIP' (tm)
Flexible thin plastic sheet material made by Dycem Ltd, with very high friction against other surfaces. An inconspicuous disk of this placed under the base of a portable lighting fitting will prevent it from slipping off a table or bedside cabinet, etc.

OPTICAL FIBRE
See *Fibre-optic light conductors*.

PAR LAMP
A type of tungsten-filament reflector lamp in a pressed-glass envelope containing an aluminised reflector which gives the lamp strong directional qualities.

PASSIVE INFRA-RED DEVICES
See *PIR device*.

PATH LIGHT
Outdoor low-mounted lighting fitting to assist pedestrian movement at night. Various types available, including low-mounted fittings in which the lamp is shielded from view and distributes its light to the ground. Other types may be almost completely buried and, with minimal protrusion above the ground, can be positioned along the centreline of the path to be followed.

PEAR SWITCH
A switch at the end of a flexible lead. Used for controlling bedside lamps, etc. See also *Torpedo switch*.

PEDESTAL LAMP
A free-standing type of floor standard, similar to but rather larger than a conventional table lamp. Not usually taller than around 1 m, and may incorporate a very large translucent shade. The term is also used for features such as a small statue holding an imitation fiery torch aloft, etc.

PELMET LIGHT
An architectural feature positioned at the head of curtains or over a window or other feature, and containing lamps (typically tubular fluorescent lamps). A pelmet light may give downward light only, or also give upward light like a cove light. See *Cove lights*.

PE SWITCH (or PE controller)
See *Photoelectric switch*.

PHOSPHOR
A chemical substance which emits visible light if irradiated with ultraviolet light. See *Fluorescent lamp*.

PHOTOELECTRIC SWITCH
Also termed a PE switch, PE controller or daylight switch. A light-sensitive switch which can be employed to turn lights on automatically at dusk and turn them off at dawn.

PICTURE LIGHT
A small lighting fitting for wall mounting containing a linear lamp (e.g. an architectural tubular lamp, a small fluorescent tubular lamp or a linear compact fluorescent lamp) mounted on a wall bracket, and designed to cast light downward to illuminate a picture while shielding the lamp from normal angles of view. In many situations, the spill light from picture lights contributes attractively to the general lighting. See page 24.

PIR DEVICE (PIR controller)
A passive infra-red detection device, separately mounted or integral to a lighting fitting, to switch it on when heat due to the presence of a person (or an animal) within its range is detected.

PROXIMITY DETECTOR
A device that detects the presence of a person, and is used to switch on lights automatically. See *PIR device*.

RADIOINTERFERENCE
From dimmers or lamp ballasts. Also called radio frequency interference or RFI. See Chapter 13.

RCD
See *Residual current device*.

RFI
See *Radiointerference*.

REFLECTOR LAMP (also called a mushroom lamp)
Typically a filament lamp with a mushroom-shaped blown-glass internally silvered reflector bulb which produces a soft-edged beam. Coloured versions are available. The term may also be applied to a PAR lamp and to an LVTH lamp.

RESIDUAL CURRENT DEVICE
A protective device which isolates a circuit from the mains when an earth-fault current occurs. See Chapter 9.

SECURITY LIGHTING
Exterior lighting which is in operation continuously

all night every night, from dusk to dawn, as a discouragement to criminals who would doubtless prefer to attack the premises under the cover of darkness.

SOCKET ADAPTOR
See Chapter 14.

STANDARD LAMP
See *Floor standard*

STARTER SWITCH (also called a starter canister)
A device that is plugged into 'switch-start' lighting fittings for fluorescent tubular lamps, and initiates the start of the lamp when switched on. Most modern fittings for fluorescent tubular lamps these days are fitted with 'switchless-start' circuits, and increasingly electronic ballasts are employed which also require no starter switch.

STRIPLIGHT
The use of this term should be avoided, for it is sometimes wrongly used to describe a tubular fluorescent lamps or an architectural lamp. (A striplight is actually a flat plastic strip containing miniature low-voltage filament lamps, and is used to mark the edge of a step in dark places like theatres and cinemas.)

SWITCH-START
A type of ballast for fluorescent tubular lamps which employs a starter canister. There is usually a second or two of delay before the lamp 'strikes', i.e. lights up. See *Starter switch.*

SWITCHLESS START
A type of ballast for fluorescent tubular lamps which does not employ a starter canister. Starting is usually faster than for switch-start ballasts. Note that electronic (high-frequency) ballasts are also 'switchless'.

TILT SWITCH
A switch fitted in a free-standing uplighter as a safety precaution. It isolates the lamp from the mains if the uplighter is tilted beyond a safe angle.

TOGGLE BOLTS (also called Butterfly bolts)
See Chapter 14.

TORPEDO SWITCH
A switch placed in the supply lead to a portable lighting fitting. See also *Pear switch.*

TOUCH-PLATE CONTROLLERS
See Chapter 14.

TRACK (also called lighting track or ceiling track)
A channel, normally for ceiling mounting, to which several spotlight or floodlight fittings may be attached, containing electric conductors to provide an electric supply to the fittings. Commonly the track incorporates a step-down transformer to provide low-voltage supplies for LVTH lamps. A track may contain more than one circuit, so that single fittings or groups of fittings mounted on it may be selectively switched or dimmed. See Chapter 14.

TRAILING SOCKET UNIT
Portable device with a number of socket outlets with a flexible cable and plug that can be inserted into a socket outlet. Features may include an additional main fuse, double-pole switching, indicators, etc. See Chapter 14.

TRANSFORMER
A device that is supplied with electric power and gives an output at a different voltage to that of the supply voltage. The output of a step-down transformer is lower than that of the input supply. Step-down transformers are used to provide supplies at 12 V for low-voltage tungsten-halogen lamps.

TRUNKING
An enclosed channel, usually rectangular in section, made of metal or plastic, which contains and protects electric wires. See *Mini-trunking.*

TUNGSTEN LAMP
See *Filament lamp.*

TH LAMP
See *Tungsten-halogen lamp.*

TUNGSTEN-HALOGEN LAMP (sometimes called a quartz-halogen lamp; formerly called a quartz-iodine lamp)

A lamp in which light is emitted from a white-hot filament of tungsten enclosed within a quartz tube. Low-power linear lamps of this type are used in wall-washer fittings and in outdoor floodlight fittings. See also *LVTH*.

TWO-POSITION SWITCHING
Also called two-way switching. See Chapter 14.

UPLIGHTER
A lighting fitting designed to direct all its light upward to the ceiling to provide indirect general lighting. An uplighter is usually free-standing on a slim column which supports a light-reflecting bowl so that its edge is above normal eye level, but wall-mounted and partition-mounted models are also available. Wall-mounted uplighters may be designed to produce an asymmetric light distribution, i.e. arranged to throw their light forward across the ceiling and not to overlight the adjacent wall and ceiling. See page 95.

WALL-WASHER
A small floodlight fitting for indoor use which is mounted at ceiling height or at the head or foot of a wall, and is designed to 'wash' the wall with light. Used mainly for decorative effect, although the light reflected diffusely from the wall provides soft general lighting in the room. See page 22.

WELLGLASS FITTING
See *Jam-jar fitting*.

2D
A pattern of compact fluorescent lamp in which a single small-diameter fluorescent tube is bent into a flat configuration similar to two capital letter Ds. *Caution:* Some cheap imported fake lamps of this kind may be on the market, and these are known to pose a fire risk. Genuine 2D lamps supplied by GE Lighting Ltd have the trademark '2D' moulded on the central polycarbonate body. See page 89.

Acknowledgements

The authors are grateful to Eric Chapman (Belvoir Lighting Consultancy) for his guidance on lighting technology, to Janine Michael (Building Research Establishment) for her guidance on energy conservation matters, and to Paul Webber (Electrical Contractors Association) for his guidance on electrical installation matters dealt with in this book. Thanks are expressed to The Lighting Association which has encouraged the preparation of this book and provided photographs, and to the following companies which have kindly provided photographs or information:

ABB-Wylex Sales Ltd
Absolute Action Ltd
Anglepoise Ltd
Arcaid
Ashley & Rock Ltd
BLE (Bradley Lomas Electrolok Ltd)
British Standards Institution
Candilejas Decorative Lighting
Crompton Lighting

C.S.M. Lighting Ltd
Dycem Ltd
Elkay Electrical Manufacturing Co. Ltd
The Garden Lighting Company
GE Lighting Ltd (Mazda)
Helvar
Interscene Ltd
John Dawes Publications
Legrand Electric Ltd
Lutron EA Ltd
Noma Lites Ltd
Noral Ltd
Osram Ltd
Philips Lighting Ltd
PowerBreaker
C. Sandberg & Sons Ltd
SLI Lighting Ltd (Linolite, Lumiance and Sylvania)
Thorn Lighting Ltd
Christopher Wray Lighting